GREENBERG'S
GUIDE TO
SUPER HERO TOYS

GREENBERG'S GUIDE

TO

SUPER HERO TOYS

Volume 1

By

Steven H. Kimball

with the assistance of John McGonagle

Photographs by

Maury Feinstein

Greenberg Publishing Company, Inc.
7566 Main Street
Sykesville, MD 21784
(301) 795-7447

First Edition

Manufactured in the United States of America

Greenberg Publishing Company, Inc. offers the world's largest selection of Lionel, American Flyer, LGB, Ives, and other toy train publications as well as a selection of books on model and prototype railroading, dollhouse miniatures, and toys. For a copy of our current catalogue, please send a large self-addressed stamped envelope to Greenberg Publishing Company, Inc. at the above address.

Greenberg Shows, Inc. sponsors the world's largest public train, dollhouse, and toy shows. They feature extravagant operating model railroads for N, HO, O, Standard, and 1 Gauges as well as a huge marketplace for buying and selling nearly all model railroad equipment. The shows also feature, a large selection of dollhouses and dollhouse furnishings. Shows are currently offered in metropolitan Baltimore, Boston, Ft. Lauderdale, Cherry Hill and Wayne in New Jersey, Long Island in New York, Norfolk, Philadelphia, Pittsburgh, and Tampa. To receive our current show listing, please send a self-addressed stamped envelope marked "Train Show Schedule" to the address above.

ISBN 0-89778-096-5

Library of Congress Cataloging-in-Publication Data

Kimball, Steven H., 1962-
    Greenberg's guide to Super hero toys / by Steven H. Kimball; with the assistance of John McGonagle. — 1st ed.
    p. cm.
    Includes index.
    ISBN 0-89778-096-5 (v. 1) : $35.00
    1. Dolls — United States — History — 20th century — Collectors and collecting — Catalogs. I. Title.
NK4894.U6K56 1988
688.7'2 — dc19   88-18055
CIP

DEDICATION

To Steve, my friend-turned-brother-in-law who,
as a fellow child, aided me in writing my first "homemade"
comic book. He never stopped enjoying heroes, even though they evolved
from **G. I. Joe** to **Dirty Harry**.
and...
To my father, who told me to stop playing with
dolls when I was nine.
and finally...
To the TV star who, in my eyes, started it all,
Adam West.

Cover Photograph: The collection of action figures on the cover represents characters from Marvel and DC Comics as well as from King Features. This colorful photograph was taken by Greenberg photographer **Maury Feinstein.** The photographer and the author spent many hours setting up the figures. When the shot was ready to be taken, the chair leg under the **Spider-Man** figure broke, sliding the figure up and off of the chair. The resulting photograph shows one of two things:

(A) Spider-Man's brute strength is winning the arm wrestle and breaking the chair in the process;

or...

(B) **Batman** is not even working up a sweat as **Spider-Man** has to break the chair and lean forward on the table.

YOU DECIDE!!

ACKNOWLEDGMENTS

From the beginning one person has kept me "punching away" at this book, constantly giving me the motivation to give equal attention to the most tedious of descriptions as well as to meaty discussions. That person is my wife, **Lari**. She deserves a citizenship award for keeping me at the typewriter.

"Thank God for this book," she often mentioned in passing. "Without Steve bothering me, I've finally earned my B. S." What is her degree in? Psychology, of course... I believe that I am a case study.

Others in my family have helped me recall my experiences with Super Hero toys. They include my mother,

From left to right are the author's wife, Lari, her sister, Terri, and their mom, Diana. All three were unexpectedly driven to Washington, D.C. by the author for a surprise visit to the Superman exhibit in the Museum of American History during the summer of 1987. S. Kimball photograph.

Marion; my younger brother, **Tom**; and most of all, my older brother, **Bob**. Bob, led me back to the 1960s when we received our **Captain Action** outfits, which we stretched over our **G. I. Joes**. Bob also aided in the editing of this manuscript.

After finishing **Greenberg's Guide to American Flyer Prewar O Gauge Trains** in August of 1987, I presented **Bruce Greenberg** with a detailed outline for a book on Super Hero toys. He agreed that it was likely that a large market for the book existed. I began the research and within a week realized that my outline for the book stretched to some 20 chapters. Consequently, we divided the contents into five volumes in order to attempt to comprehensively list and describe every Super Hero toy.

When telling collectors about my plans to list and describe every Super Hero toy, I received replies such as "... can't be done," "Sure, what are you selling?" and "Good luck!" followed by sarcastic chuckles.

But three individuals spoke differently and motivated my research: **John McGonagle**, **Jim Carlo**, and **Jim Main**. These individuals continue to confront me with new ideas, explanations, and hundreds of Super Hero toy variations.

John McGonagle and I, singlehandedly, kept the phone company in business. With all of our lengthy long-distance discussions, we probably put an AT&T executive's child through college. John's knowledge of **Captain Action** still leaves me speechless. He put at least a hundred man-hours into reviewing and correcting my initial manuscript. Besides **Captain Action**, he also improved every draft of the manuscript, spewing out variations and action figures that I never knew existed.

John also invited staff photographer, **Maury Feinstein**, and me to his house to photograph his collection. We photographed all of the **Captain Action** items, but only scratched the surface of his Super Hero memorabilia. Upon entering his toy room, it became apparent that **Batman** was his favorite character. We will call upon John again and again for in-depth research as the volumes progress.

Jim Main, an enthusiastic **Captain Action** collector as well as the Managing Editor for "Spotlight Comics," also assisted in editing this manuscript. They say that every author needs an editor, no matter how well he writes. Without changing my thoughts or context, Jim managed to wade his way through my haphazard writing style and gently edited the text to produce a careful and consistent piece of workmanship. He deserves much credit.

Jim Carlo was the first to assist me. His expertise about **Super Powers** and **Secret Wars** is incredible. He also gave constructive comments on every chapter.

The "Mego-Man" himself, **Mark Huckabone**, labored for weeks over his large collection of Mego figures. Mark's collection not only includes Super Heroes, but **Star Trek**, **Wizard of Oz**, **Planet of the Apes**, and various TV series' figures made by Mego. His eight-inch Mego figures are a universe unto themselves. Mark has one of every figure in that universe and two of most figures!

Thanks are also extended to Lionel toy train enthusiasts and copy editors, **Pete Riddle** and **Ken Starke**. No author has ever enjoyed two such easy-to-work-with editors.

Ted Hake, the first toy dealer to help, made available many of the photographs in this volume as well as others to come. Ted lent a dozen of his auction catalogues so that I could choose 50 photographs to use. **Ted's Auction House** is a great place to begin a collection. His address is listed in Appendix II.

The wonderful dealer that I have worked with in building my collection is **Barbara Andresen** (a.k.a. **CHERIB**). She provided information about various manufacturers and is very knowledgeable about the doll world.

Joe Desris and **Danny Fuchs** are specialists and authors in their own rights. Joe is *the* **Batman** expert. DC Comics has called upon him many times in locating licensing of the **Batman** character. He helped me a great deal by adding information from his own collection.

Danny Fuchs, who is known as "America's Foremost **Superman** Collector," collaborated on a wonderful, full-color, coffee table-type book entitled, *The Adventures of Superman Collecting*. I recommend it for its information about **Superman** toys. That book is the reason that the **Superman** character is barely touched upon in these volumes. With the wealth of information on **Superman**, it would be a duplication of effort to list all the toys. **Danny** has shared information on some of the most popular **Superman** toys.

Another dealer, **Steve Maged**, traveled to Europe to gather sets of rare **Secret Wars** figures and returned with a special set of European-made Marvel figures that were unknown to American collectors. Steve also helped edit the manuscript and provided many figures to be photographed.

The man known to me only as **Dan**, who works at Geppi's Comic World (my comic book haunt), also read the manuscript and noted corrections regarding the comic book material. He and others at Geppi's are to be thanked.

Craig Hedges lent me photos and information regarding **Captain Action**. His stockpile of **Captain Action** paper was very helpful to back up discussions in that chapter.

Collector **Jim Makowski** also aided in the works concerning **Captain Action** and some of his collection is shown in that chapter. Jim provided us with a never-before-seen **Captain Action** sales poster that also appears later in the book.

The President of **Other Worlds Collectibles**, Frank R. **Pacella**, aided my discussion of **Captain Action** and the Mego figures.

Samuel Baum (Sam, to his friends), a fellow staff editor and comic book collector, shared his knowledge of comic book Super Heroes; his help was a major contribution.

Captain Bijou or **Earl Blair** also corresponded and shared his knowledge of the video market.

Another Super-Hero collector, **Mike Curtis** (with one of the largest **Superman** collections), also helped with various chapters.

George Acevedo enlightened me on various toys from Mego to Remco. He also acted as an editor and lent a few Super Hero toy catalogues.

Dale L. Ames, probably the most knowledgeable collector of **Captain Midnight and the Galaxy Patrol**, gave me interesting information for this and other volumes.

At **Greenberg Publishing**, there were many who contributed to this book.

No one was more helpful than **Maury Feinstein**, who photographed most items appearing in this volume. He and I spent many hours just to arrange the characters to stand up for the cover photograph. He traveled with me up and down the east coast in our quest to photograph every Super Hero collection. Without Maury, the book would have lost much of its character (sorry for the pun) and I am greatly in his debt.

In additon, **Donna Price** proofread all of the copy and **Cindy Lee Floyd**, **Linda Greenberg**, **Leslie Greenberg**, and **Carole Norbeck** provided much editorial assistance. **Maureen Crum**, **Sam Baum**, and I designed the book's final format. This book has the added bonus of being the first Greenberg publication to be completed using a laser printer.

Finally, my sincere thanks to **Bruce** and **Linda Greenberg** who thought my idea to write a book on Super Hero toys of great merit, although they themselves knew nothing of the field. Their trust in me and in the culmination of this effort has been truly gratifying.

I know now that a book of any size is an upward struggle. The exciting parts included book research, correspondence, and talking with fellow collectors. The tedious part was listing all of this information and molding a manuscript from a maze of statistics. Without the dedication of all concerned, the book never would have been published. I thank you all.

STEVEN H. KIMBALL
Sykesville, Maryland
July, 1988

Table of Contents

HOW TO USE THIS GUIDE

The development of the contemporary toy market has occurred very rapidly. Thousands and thousands of people collect toys from the sixties, seventies, and eighties. The market for these toys has created a common understanding of the value of most contemporary toys. This book reports the Super Hero market data.

However, as with all markets, there are short-term value fluctuations. It is important to study and understand these processes. For example, in 1986 the Kenner Toys **Super Powers Green Arrow** action figure was moderately successful. However in 1987 DC Comics introduced a new **Green Arrow** in a different costume and, consequently, the demand for **Green Arrow** figures increased four-fold. This increased popularity drove the price up accordingly.

Another example is the ever-popular **Superman**. Though licenses to manufacture **Superman** toys have long been in demand, **Superman** toys substantially increased in value last year when he celebrated his 50th birthday. (The man ages like Dick Clark!) However, by next year **Superman** figures' values may drop like a Kryptonite meteor. This year, **Batman** toys' popularity could surge because **Batman** celebrates his 50th birthday, and because *BATMAN: THE MOVIE* is due to be released in late 1989.

Value is also strongly related to availability on toy shelves. After toys are no longer available from toy retailers, there is a tendency for prices to go up. In your area, you might still make a good purchase of the Galoob toys **Defenders of the Earth** from a local retailer. But in other parts of the country, the toys are not available and have appreciated in value! It is possible, though unlikely, that you might pick up an entire Ideal toys **Captain Action** collection at a yard sale for a pittance; yet if you bought these items separately from someone who knows the value of **Captain Action**, you would shell out a great deal of cash.

No matter how old or new these toys are, they share two common traits: They are all very attractive and are likely to increase in value. In fact, Super Hero toys are more available now than they have been for the past twenty years, since they are available from secondary markets — garage sales and flea markets — as well as at retail stores.

Toy appreciation is also related to toy manufacture. Some toys are more durable than others. Toys which break easily are harder to find in excellent condition, and these consequently will likely rise more rapidly in price than a more durable toy.

Prices reflect the desires of collectors. If some items are wanted by more collectors than other items, the wanted items' prices will rise. This book will help bring more order to the Super Hero marketplace by sharing the existing commonly shared perceptions.

NOTE TO BUYERS

The following comments will assist you in becoming an informed buyer.

Super Hero toy collecting is fun and can be inexpensive. If you collect toys from a broad category (i.e., Super Hero action figures) and not a specialty (i.e., Marvel **Secret Wars Iceman Secret Shield** inserts), you can usually find toys at a reasonable price or less at every flea market or yard sale (with any luck at all, and virtually no effort). But buying a broad range of toys is not a good strategy for maximizing the appreciation of your collection.

After you discover what you want to collect, find the time to list what you want and cross-reference it with your checkbook. Even rare item collectibles can be collected on a modest budget, if you save your funds and make less frequent purchases. It is very important for peace of mind and good family relationships that you establish your priorities and a budget. Spending too much of your income on toys can lead to very unfortunate circumstances and destroy the pleasures and joys of toy collecting. An acquaintance of mine once told me that he "could not eat" his comic books and had to sell his entire collection to pay the rent.

Do some research in local newspapers by checking out auctions, flea markets, and what has become the collector's Godsend: yard and garage sales! Visit an Americana-type museum that has contemporary toys, although unfortunately, most Americana museums do not yet have toys from the 1960s and 1970s, but they will! Auctions are fun to visit. I would recommend that a newcomer not bid but absorb all the information that the auction provides. Flea markets, church bazaars, and yard and garage sales all offer a wide range of toys at low prices.

A common mistake of the inexperienced Super Hero toy buyer is to buy one of each item. A better strategy is to buy two or three of any inexpensive collectible you can. An experienced collector would much rather trade an item for one he needs than sell one from his collection. I know several **Captain Action** collectors who will *not* sell from their collections, but will willingly trade for something they need (like a **Captain Action Green Hornet** costume!).

So you think you have seen it all! From auctions to museums you have seen hundreds of toys and you have decided what you'll pay for those you want. Next, gather your resources and courage and attend a toy show! A toy show is the last bastion of old-fashioned marketplace bartering. To a knowledgeable collector, the toy show is his most exciting and challenging arena. It provides the novice with the opportunity to observe experienced collectors who are in the process of building their collections bargaining with dealers. From calm transactions to the crying pleas of die-hard cheapskates, the toy show is the collector's Wall Street.

I was lucky enough to participate in this collector's "tribal ritual" for two days at a local **Greenberg's Great Train, Dollhouse and Toy Show**. I manned a display booth with my wife and witnessed first-hand the excitement of the marketplace. We attended the show to promote this book, and I brought my collection of **Super Powers** and **Secret Wars** figures for display. The show provoked radically different responses ranging from: *"This toy show was a great place to bring the kids and keep them busy."* to: *"Why do people insist on bringing kids to purchase toys that will be broken in ten minutes...especially when they buy the toys that I want to collect!"*

There was a general atmosphere of both fun and frolic, as well as intense bartering. New collectors should not be put off by the intense show atmosphere. At the same time they should be advised that professional dealers sometimes lie in wait for the novice! As with auctions, your first show should include more looking than buying. Take notes and file them away.

Other types of marketplaces are mail auctions and mail order catalogues. In the case of the mail auction, you decide what you want, write up a bid, attach a check, either as a deposit or for the full amount, and send it off. In a month or so, a notice arrives stating either that you bid too low (in which case you receive a refund) or that your merchandise is attached, or a request to send the balance for your merchandise. Mail auctions involve a large element of chance. If you are too exuberant, you may pay too much. Or you might bid too low for something you have desperately wanted. There are several fine mail order auction houses listed in the back of this volume.

The mail order catalogue, especially one with photographs, is one of the easiest sources for purchasing collectibles. You simply get a catalogue (from a trade newspaper or a friend), call in what you want, and send your money. Calling your order in insures your purchase and gives you personal contact with a dealer. The friendlier you are, the more the dealer will help you. In most cases, if you send the dealer a "want list" along with how much you will pay for an item, the dealer will set those things aside and a reasonable deal can be arranged.

In summing up, the best approach is starting slowly and buying lightly until you become more knowledgeable and experienced. There are *plenty* of toys out there! With a price guide such as this one to help you, your new (or old) hobby can be the most relaxing, enjoyable, and satisfying entertainment available, and you might even turn a profit!

USING THIS GUIDE

Purpose

The purpose of this book is to provide a comprehensive listing with current prices for Super Hero toy action figures produced from the 1930s through 1988. In a few cases we ask our readers for further information where information is missing or doubtful. Values are reported for each item where there have been reported sales.

Determining Values

Toy values in this book are based on *obtained* prices, rather than asking prices, along the East Coast during the summer of 1988. We have chosen East Coast prices since the greatest dollar volume in transactions appears there. The prices reported here represent a "ready sale," or a price perceived as a good value by the buyer. They may sometimes appear lower than those seen on toys at shows for two reasons. First, items that sell often do so in the first hour of a toy show and therefore are no longer visible. We have observed that a good portion of the action at most shows occurs in the first hour. The items that do not sell in the first hour have a higher price tag and this price, although not representing the sales price, is the price observed. A related source of discrepancy is the willingness of some sellers to bargain over price.

Another factor which may affect prices is dealer reconditioning. Some dealers take great pains to clean and service their toys so that they look their best. Others sell the items just as they have acquired them, dust and all. Naturally, the more effort the dealer expends in preparing his toys for sale, the more he can expect to charge for them. This factor may account for significant price differences among dealers selling the same toys.

From our studies of toy prices, it appears that mail order prices for used toys are generally higher than those obtained at Eastern toy shows. This is appropriate considering the cost and effort of producing and distributing a price list and packing and shipping items. Mail order items do sell at prices above those listed in this book. A final source of difference between observed prices and reported prices is region. Prices are clearly higher in the South and West where collectable toys are less plentiful than along the East Coast.

Condition

For each item, we provide two categories: **Very Good** and **Mint**. We define these conditions as:

VERY GOOD: Few scratches, exceptionally clean, no dents or rust.

MINT: Brand new, absolutely unmarred, all original and unused, in original box.

Pricing Codes

CR — CURRENT RETAIL: The item is readily available for purchase from current dealer stocks. The price fluctuates somewhat according to exchange rate, the seller's cost basis, and local competition.

NRS — NO REPORTED SALES: In the few cases where there is insufficient information upon which to determine the value of a given item, we show **NRS** in the price column. Here again we recommend that you rely on your **experience** or on the **assistance** of an experienced collector to determine what price you should pay for any of these items.

TBA — TO BE ANNOUNCED: Item is being produced but has not yet been shipped from the factory.

There is substantial confusion in the minds of both sellers and buyers as to what constitutes "**mint**" condition. How do we define mint? Among very experienced toy enthusiasts, a mint toy means that it is brand new, in its original box, and extremely bright and clean (and the box is, too). An item may have been removed from the box and replaced in it but it should show no evidence of handling. A toy is not mint if it shows any scratches, fingerprints, or evidence of discoloration. It is the nature of a market for the seller to see his item in a very positive light and to seek to obtain a mint price for a very good toy. In contrast, a buyer will see the same item in a less favorable light and will attempt to buy a mint toy for the price of one in very good condition. It is our responsibility to point out this difference in perspective **and** the difference in value implicit in each perspective, and to then let the buyer and seller settle or negotiate their different perspectives.

We do not show values for **Good**, **Fair**, or **Restored**. **Fair** items are valued substantially below **Good**. We have not included **Restored** because such items are not a significant portion of the market for Super Hero toys. As a rough guide, however, we expect that **Restored** items will bring prices equivalent to **Good** or possibly **Very Good**. The term professional restoration refers to highly proficient technical work. There is some disagreement among restorers as to what constitutes appropriate technique and finished product. There are substantial differences in the prices that consumers are willing to pay for restored items.

As we indicated, prices in this book were derived from large toy shows, dealers, and collectors. If you have toys to sell and you sell them to a person planning to resell them, you will not obtain the prices reported in this book. Rather, you should expect to achieve about fifty percent of these prices. Basically, for your items to be of interest to a buyer who plans to resell them, he must purchase them for considerably less than the prices listed here.

New Variations and Corrections

If you wish to report a new entry, variation, or correction to us, please write to:

Greenberg Publishing Company, Inc.
Guide to Super Hero Toys
7566 Main Street
Sykesville, Maryland 21784

We appreciate very much your cooperation, enthusiasm, and good will in helping us document Super Hero toy production. As has been our custom, we will acknowledge all varieties noted in the Guide as coming from your collection and/or observation.

COLLECTING SUPER HEROES

A History and Introduction

You will discover in this brief introduction the unbelievable power of the mass media. The Super Hero has moved from newspapers and comic books to radio, movies, and television. Today's Super Hero is the product of mass merchandising in mass media, usually aimed at the male child from 6 to 12 years old. Children have been, and will continue to be, the key decision makers in the fate of toys and toy manufacturers. It reminds me of **Wimpy** coaxing **Swee' Pea**, while in transit to a horse race, into guessing the winning nag.

This Guide does not cover science fiction or space characters, with some exceptions. They are **Flash Gordon** and **Buck Rogers**, two early science fiction heroes; **Superman**, who has extra-terrestrial origins but operates on an earthly basis; the **Green Hornet**; **Captain Midnight**; **Captain Video**; and others.

PRE-1966

In 1896 a new journalistic tool was invented: the cartoon strip. The first cartoon strip was called **The Yellow Kid** and was created by Richard Outcault. Also in that year, Rudolf Dirks created the very popular **Katzenjammer Kids**.

From the **Katzenjammer Kids** came Fred Opper's **Happy Hooligan** in 1900 and in 1915, Fontaine Fox originated the **Toonerville Folks** whose **Toonerville Trolley** remains the most remembered comic-turned-toy of the era.

During the Depression children were warned to be thrifty with their money and to purchase toys that would last. What did they buy?.... comic books, which after trading on top of trading had a life span of about two to three days. The big collectable item in those days was the baseball card, because anyone could get a ten-cent comic book, but not everyone had a vintage Babe Ruth!

During the 1930s comics usually came in three genres: Crime (featuring various G-men and their criminal counterparts), Humor, and Horror. Most of the remaining comic categories were folk heroes such as Robin Hood or tales of the Old West.

This all changed when **Superman**, the first Super Hero, appeared in the comics in 1938. High schoolers Joe Shuster and Jerry Siegel were the fathers of the Super Hero, and for the last 50 years **Superman** has been the most widely-known Super Hero in the world. This bigger-than-life hero was followed by **Captain Marvel**, the **Sub-Mariner**, **Batman**, **Hawkman**, **Sheena**, **Flash**, and the **Human Torch**.

All or most of these heroes had their following. In those days, all you needed in order to have a Super Hero toy was a red towel and *"Ta-Daa"*... you were **Superman**. Thus, before the advent of the Super Hero toy, came American child-ingenuity.

During the 1930s and 1940s, radio was in its heyday, and tales of the **Green Hornet** and **Captain Midnight**, as well as many other "dramas of the mind," were literally comic books read into a microphone. World War II ushered in a search for more heroes. **Captain America**, **Wonder Woman**, the first **Daredevil**, and others arrived and collectively ended the war. Who can forget the **Human Torch's** duel with the Nazis which ended only when Hitler's bunker was burned to cinders?

Captain Marvel, first illustrated in 1940 by C. C. Beck, became a movie serial star in 1941. Fifteen chapters told the story of *The Adventures of* **Captain Marvel***, the World's Mightiest Mortal*. Here the movies brought the comic book Super Hero to life, and set the stage for even more merchandising. In 1949, **"Captain Video"** appeared on television, marking the first Super Hero on TV. A similar serial ran in 1951.

By 1950, Super Heroes were no longer a comic book mainstay. This was the atomic age and a time for comic books to look to an exciting future. (At that time, we "knew" that the future would be entirely neon and that automobiles would fly on nuclear power.) Comic books said good-bye to most heroes and hello to Science Fiction, Horror, Fantasy, and Crime. A few Super Heroes survived. **Superman** still feared kryptonite, **Batman** became more of a detective, and the **Green Hornet** came back, this time without the 1930s-style G-Men.

1956 saw D. C. National revitalize its comic books by bringing back its 1940s' heroes to deal with the fiendish nuclear criminals of a modern age. The next landmark came in 1965 when the **Fantastic Four** carried Marvel comics to fame and fortune. The following year, Stan (the Man) Lee introduced **Thor, Hulk**, and the very popular **Spider-Man**.

1966

Why single out 1966?

To explain, we have to take a trip back in time. In 1966 on a typical Wednesday evening, you've just gotten up from dinner and are sitting down in front of the new color TV. How wonderful it is to see fantasy come to life, in technicolor, without having to pay a dollar or two at the movie theater. It is 7:30 pm (Prime Time), January 12th, and you are about to witness a comic book Super Hero come to life like never before.... "**BATMAN!**" That night marked the beginning of a super-fad which changed the then dim prospects for Super Heroes.

From that moment on, **BATMAN!** became the definitive Super Hero; he was what some label a "camp-humorest" with cameos of various movie and TV stars helping his rise to fame. In doing so, some claim, the show forever altered the American Super Hero. To this day, older comic-collectors, who remember the World War II likes of **Captain America, Superman**, and **Captain Midnight**, cannot take the post-1966 **Batman** seriously.

Thanks to the creative efforts at DC Comics, **Batman** is again receiving his due, as both Super Hero and master detective.

But, in 1966, this was not the case. According to those involved with "**BATMAN!**," the show's success stemmed from the marriage of an audience of adults and children. This rare combination saw mutual escape during a period of what some refer to as "mindlessness." The 1960s reveled in the fantasy of finding what you sought. The adults enjoyed the humor and the children really got into "**BATMAN!**"'s aura and effects.

When **Batman** first appeared, DC Comics' (then called National Periodicals) stock rose ten points a month for the first year and then stabilized. But the success of the comic book did not equal the huge success of the TV show.

Not everyone saw the success and fun of this America-encompassing program in the same light. The Soviet media accused "**BATMAN!**" of "brainwashing Americans into becoming willing murderers in the Vietnam Jungle." "**Batman** and **Robin** look like idealized representations of the F. B. I." they wrote and they blamed the show for other American difficulties.

In researching "**BATMAN!**," from sources such as *The Batbook*, by Joel Eisner, and *Pop Sixties*, by Andrew J. Edelstein, various facts about the TV show became evident.

The character Aunt Harriet rarely appeared in the comic book but was written into the TV show's cast. According to Executive Producer William Dozier, Aunt Harriet was added to keep the dynamic duo and their butler from looking homosexual! "**BATMAN!**" was nominated only once for an Emmy. In 1966, the program was nominated for Individual Achievements in Sound Editing. The show was one of the most expensive TV shows to produce at that time. A great deal of money was spent on the optical effects of superimposing the "BAMMs" and "KA-POWW"s that were edited into the fight scenes! The crooked camera angles used in most of the scenes reflected the panel designs of the comic book!

With all of the ruckus of the TV show came the Bat-Fad. The Bat-Fad took the United States by storm. From Bat-T-shirts to Bat-hand grenade toys, you can still find Bat-memorabilia in just about any fashion.

Collecting Bat-memorabilia soon led to Super-memorabilia and Spider-memorabilia as each Super Hero took his turn on "the tube." Whether right after school or early Saturday mornings, TV moved the Super Hero from comic book to living room. With each show came a popular figure or toy which is what this volume is about, changing this literature from book to time capsule.

THE 1970S

During this decade, television introduced the "**Six-Million Dollar Man**," whom we have not listed as a Super Hero because he was more of a cyborg-spy. **Wonder Woman** (the original pilot with Cathy Lee Crosby) and **Spider-Man** also came to television with less than fantastic results. The only TV programs in this vein to last were "**Buck Rogers in the 25th Century**," "**The Incredible Hulk**," and "**Wonder Woman**" (with Linda Carter). There were other TV pilots that did not go over too well, namely, "**Doc Savage**," "**Captain America**," "**Doctor Strange**," "**Mandrake the Magician**," and recently, "**The Spirit**."

We also cannot forget the live-action Saturday morning Super Heroes "**SHAZAM!**" featuring the original **Captain Marvel** and a new character, **Isis**. The Saturday morning cartoons are discussed in the 1970s section. Meanwhile in the movie theaters, we were repelled by a new version of *Flash Gordon* and delighted by *Superman* (though later sequels of the *Superman* series were disappointing). Recently, comic book fans have been strung along with rumors of movies involving **The Silver Surfer**, **Batman**, and no less than the **Fantastic Four** and **Daredevil**.

In the last ten years, Marvel and DC Comics have dominated the comic book scene and, with the advent of comic book stores (which specialize in comic books and their paraphrenalia only), Super Hero toys have been brought to the attention of comic character lovers.

Within this and later volumes, you will be delighted by all the Super Hero toys you've grown to love. Each volume includes color plates, black and white photographs, in-depth toy descriptions, and prices, as well as articles on specific types of toys, and curious facts that you won't find anywhere else. As an extra bonus, a ready reference guide to all of the characters used more than twice as action figures, their discriptions, and copyright holders of the character is included. Each character discription is referenced to four illustrations.

So, put on your red cape (you know, the one with the big yellow "S" on it), and pull up a chair.

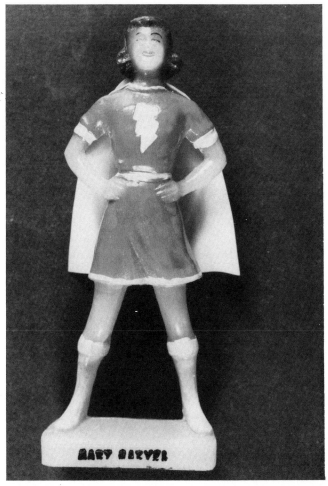 

The statues of Mary Marvel and Marvel Bunny as they look now. These plastic figures "in realistic colors!" came four to a package. Also in this set were Captain Marvel and Captain Marvel, Jr. Photos courtesy of Hake's Americana and Collectibles.

LESS THAN ACTION FIGURES

As noted in the Introduction, the media played a major role in the marketing of Super Heroes. It is also obvious that Super Heroes' origins can be traced to comic strips and comic books in particular. Daily contact as well as the comics' exciting story line mark the beginnings of this tale of collectable Super Hero action figures. Tons of toys were licensed as Super Heroes. Great care has been taken to define and compile a listing that is neither too wordy nor too general.

• This volume contains "action figures" only. Action figures are bendable at any or all of the following anatomical features: head, shoulders, elbows, wrists, hips, knees, and ankles. Some other "statues" and unarticulated figures are discussed, as references or in miscellaneous listings. Listed separately with values are action figures that were comic book or media-related Super Heroes first and toys second. **He-Man**, **Thundercats**, and **MASK** are therefore excluded. The exception to this rule is **Captain Action**.

• Super Heroes live in the civilized "modern" era and wear outlandish costumes or possess special powers that normal men do not. Therefore, **Tarzan**, **Conan**, or **Sheena** are excluded. Exceptions are those non-powered Super Heroes who appear in groups, such as the **Phantom** in the **Defenders of the Earth**. A few space heroes are treated as Super Heroes because of their close ties to Super Heroes.

(**Buck Rogers** is an Earthman in space and **Superman** is an alien on Earth!)

With these boundaries in mind, let us return to the past in order to study the predecessors of the modern action figure, when Super Hero statues were great fun to play with and no one minded their being "rooted to the spot."

During the 1930s children played with numerous lead figures, featuring various characters from **Buck Rogers** to **Flash Gordon**. These figures, some manufactured by Tootsietoy, were usually 1-3/4" tall and fully-molded. Many figures, after casting, were hand-filed, polished, embossed, and painted, and their high quality makes them valuable today. The figures were either sold as sets, as in the case of Tootsietoy, with a silver-colored space rocket, or as radio premiums, as in the case of the Cocomalt figures. The Cocomalt premiums were quite successful advertising tools in their day. Each Cocomalt figure came sealed in cellophane with an enclosed listing of times and frequencies for major cities' radio programs. These figures are sometimes worth up to $300 each in mint, unopened packages.

This Captain Video package contains a figure of Captain Video and a whistling rocket ship. S. Kimball Collection.

Due to the emergence of Super Heroes, as well as the new plastic mold injection technology, even more statues and figures appeared in a wide variety of characters during the 1940s.

As popular as **Superman** was, the original **Captain Marvel (SHAZAM!)** was just as well received. In fact, as **Superman** had his family, so did **Captain Marvel**.

In 1946 Fawcett marketed (through an unidentified manufacturer) a box of four characters of the **Marvel** family. **Captain Marvel** at a towering 6-1/2" tall was the largest and the others descended in size by age. The most humorous, and rarest, of the four was **Marvel Bunny**. Each had traditional colors from the comics but **Captain Marvel** seemed to resemble more actor Tom Tyler, who played **Captain Marvel** in the serial, than the character from the comics.

The box for the Flying Captain Marvel figure. Though not an action figure by our standards, the toy provided a lot of action for those who could afford the ten cent price! Photo courtesy Hake's Americana and Collectibles.

A 1940s **Superman** carnival figure was 15" tall, molded of plaster, and was originally brightly colored, but when found today, the colors have usually faded. Of the many photos of these figures I have seen in various collections, not one is the same as any other. Perhaps the carnival companies added decorations to the figures just to make sure that their prizes were different from those offered at the previous carnival. Some of the decorations included different paint schemes, cloth capes, and randomly-applied glitter!

MISCELLANEOUS PRE-1960s LISTINGS

TOOTSIETOY BUCK ROGERS: 1930s; miniature 1-3/4" tall, fully-molded and nicely-detailed figure with "Buck" on bottom of base; figure was issued with Tootsietoy rockets; solid silver finish. Hake's Americana and Collectibles.   **100   200**

TOOTSIETOY WILMA (Buck Rogers Series): 1930s; same series as above; finished in solid gold color. Hake's Americana and Collectibles.   **50   75**

FLASH GORDON FIGURE: 1944; 5" tall fully-dimensional wood composition figure with name on front of base; light blue shirt, yellow hair; flesh-toned face and hands;

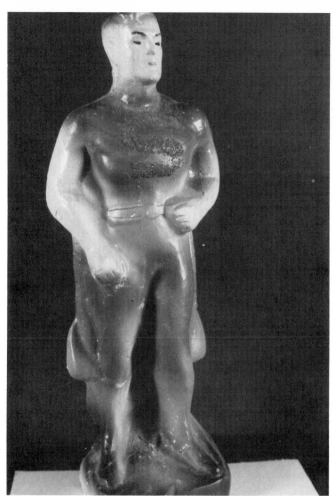

A Superman carnival figure of the 1940s in which no two carnival companies had identical figures. Photo courtesy of Hake's Americana and Collectibles.

the lower part of the figure and base were natural wood color and the added colors were original. Back of base had 1944 King Features Syndicate copyright. Hake's Americana and Collectibles. **100** **200**

SUPERMAN CARNIVAL FIGURE: 1940s; 15" tall molded plaster figure. **Superman** collector Danny Fuchs says that these figures had a molded round back showing the cape. The most valuable of these statues had the **Superman** "S" symbol molded into the chest while the plaster was still soft.

(A) Front of figure was fully-dimensional and extremely colorful; uniform in unusual dark green with traditional red stockings, briefs, and cape. Face and hands were flesh-toned, extending up arms and blending with green of the uniform at shoulders. On his chest was a glitter "S", although glitter was usually dark; body colors blended into a soft black at the base and hair, eyebrows, and eyelines were also black; figure's colors were blended softly by spray technique and paint was missing its gloss on his fists. Hake's Americana and Collectibles. **50** **100**

(B) Identical to (A), but with flat, unfinished back. **NRS**

COCOMALT BUCK ROGERS: 2-1/2" factory-painted lead figure of **Buck Rogers**; sealed in cellophane, with blue and white paper listing the radio information. Hake's Americana and Collectibles. **50** **100**

SYROCO FIGURES: 1940s; approximately 5" tall with name on front of base and King Features copyright on back of base.

(A) **Flash Gordon** — no additional details known. Hake's Americana and Collectibles. **50** **100**

(B) **Phantom** — no additional details known. Hake's Americana and Collectibles. **50** **100**

BUCK ROGERS LEAD FIGURE: 1935-36; 1-7/8" tall, silver-colored figure; detailed and fully-dimensional with "BUCK" on the bottom of base. Hake's Americana and Collectibles. **25** **50**

JOINTED SUPERMAN FIGURE (IDEAL): 1939; 13" tall figure with composition head and upper torso; wooden arms and lower body. Traditional uniform with wooden fists and composition head; jointed at neck, shoulders, elbows, wrists, waist, thighs, and knees, boot tops and ankles. Hake's Americana and Collectibles. **50** **100**

COMPLETE SET OF FOUR ALL-PLASTIC MARVEL FAMILY STATUETTES: 1946; boxes in full color and lettered with the names of the family members and "Boys! Girls! Here's What You've Been Waiting For! Lifelike Plastic Models Of The Famous Marvel Family (In Realistic Colors)." The four statues stood on bases about 1-1/2" x 2-1/2". **Captain Marvel** was 6-1/2" tall and the others were about 6". Each unpainted plastic base along with the unpainted areas of their legs, arms, hands, and heads was a dark beige. Each statue had the character's name in black lettering on the base front edge and the Fawcett 1946 copyright on the base back edge. Each wore a traditional costume and had colored facial details. A manufacturers decal was under the base. Set included **Captain Marvel**, **Mary Marvel**, **Captain Marvel, Jr.**, and **Marvel Bunny**. Priced by the set. Hake's Americana and Collectibles.

200 **400**

Of course, these are but a few of the hundreds of toys made as Super Heroes. **Superman** collectibles alone warrant their own book. A fellow collector, the heralded "America's Foremost **Superman** Collector," Danny Fuchs, has collaborated on a beautiful book, *The Adventures of Superman Collecting.* Joe Desris, fanatical **Batman** collector, is planning a similar book about the Caped Crusader.

Both have shown me the impressive amount of information and collectibles licensed for just these two heroes. Thus, this and following volumes will discuss a few of the special toys based on major characters such as **Batman**, **Superman**, and **Spider-Man**, while still providing a grand look at Super Hero toys, in general.

While helping to edit *GREENBERG'S GUIDE TO MARX TOYS, Volume I,* by Maxine Pinsky, I dis-

The Marx Superman Turnover Tank, a very popular collectable toy.

covered many beautifully lithographed Super Hero tin toys of the 1940s-1950s. For example, the Marx Turnover Tank with its attached **Superman** is one of two Marx tin **Superman** toys of the 1940s. The other pits **Superman** against the then latest weapon of modern technology, an airplane. Anyone who has seen the Max Fleisher **Superman** cartoons of the 1940s will notice their resemblance in color and atmosphere to the Marx toys.

I cannot stress enough the beauty of the colored lithography on the tin toys of the 1940s. Unique to these toys is the attention to detail, such as rivets on the plane or small wheels on the tank. It is not surprising that these two Marx toys are exremely sought-after and valuable. Further information about these two toys will appear in Volume II.

If we have omitted your favorite Super Hero toy (or worse yet, your favorite Super Hero), please write to us and we will try to include it in our next edition.

Now, we take you to 1966. Here, you will see a marketing wonder that not only made the Ideal Toy Company rich, but gave warring comic book companies an even shake as characters from both companies were represented... by only one figure!

Captain Action, the definitive Super Hero figure of the late 1960s, is garbed in his traditional uniform. Next to him is the first issue box. J. McGonagle Collection.

IDEAL — CAPTAIN ACTION

With the assistance of John McGonagle

INTRODUCTION

A 1966 Ideal Toy advertisement reads: *"You'll thrill to endless adventures with these mighty men of action! Captain Action is the brave new hero you can pose in 1,001 action positions. Change his face mask and uniform and he's Batman, fighting crime with his batarang. Change him again and he's Superman, flying to the rescue. You can change him into nine of your favorite Super Heroes!"*

Therein lies the most accurate description of **Captain Action, (C.A.)**, the 12" posable action figure made by Ideal from 1966-68

As described in the introduction, 1966 was a landmark year for Super Heroes who appeared on

G. I. Joe compared to Captain Action. Notice both are roughly the same height. J. McGonagle Collection.

Captain Action's Lightning Sword for "quick-silver assaults." J. McGonagle Collection.

THE FIGURE

Captain Action's injection-molded plastic body was jointed at the shoulders, elbows, wrists, hips, knees, and ankles. His hands were molded with open palms and pointed index fingers to hold a gun. **C. A.'s** hands were much more realistic than the two-fingered **G. I. Joe** who always looked like he was reaching for chopsticks. If you have ever tried to put a pistol or rifle trigger into **G. I. Joe's** two-fingered hand, you understand the hand design's problem. The rest of **C. A.'s** body was unremarkable and was similar to **G. I. Joe's**, featuring a well-toned muscular build.

C. A. was issued in four different boxes during his "life span." The first box had a painting of **Captain Action** in an action pose and had smaller pictures of the nine characters he could become on the right-hand side and box top. The second box was basically the same except that the picture of the shirt of the **Lone Ranger** (a character which **C. A.** could change into) was blue, while the first box showed him in a red shirt. The third issue **Captain Action** box from 1967 was the same. This doll came with a free parachute. A printed yellow box announced the parachute offer at the top of the carton. The fourth issue box from 1968 was identical to the first issue, but this time the box top showed a photo cover of **Captain Action** standing over **Dr. Evil**, with **Action Boy** in the background.

both television and in comic books. The Super Hero craze that ensued followed the massive popularity of the "**BATMAN!**" TV series. At that time, Hasbro's **G. I. Joe** had a firm "kung-fu" grip on the action figure market which included an almost infinite number of accessories. **G. I. Joe** was the first action figure to have an outfit and a weapon to fight any and every threat to America. From a detailed one-man Mercury capsule (that resembled the Gemini command module) to a battery-operated jeep, **G. I. Joe** won the heart of every child in the country. Many girls had **G. I. Joe** accessory collections, though the uniforms looked silly on **Barbie** dolls.

In order to break Hasbro's hold on the market, Ideal launched **Captain Action**, a Super Hero for any occasion. **Captain Action** seemed to parallel **G. I. Joe** in the types of small accessories, such as guns, helmets, etc..., that were manufactured, but there were very few large **Captain Action** accessories.

This close-up of Captain Action and G. I. Joe's hands shows the difference in realism. J. McGonagle Collection.

Captain Action came in four different boxes. From left to right: his introduction in 1966, the second issue box, the third issue box with free parachute in 1967, and the photo box of late 1967. J. McGonagle Collection.

The only other difference between the first two boxes was the cardboard's weight: the first issue box was made of very strong cardboard and later in the year the company switched to a lighter weight cardboard. The original **Captain Action** uniform was blue and black with the triangular red, green, and yellow **C. A.** logo in the center. He doffed a removable, blue combination cap with an anchor centered over the silver-braided brim.

He wore black Type 1A plastic boots with horizontal lightning bolts stretching from the pointed top of

The two sides of the Captain Action Videomatic ring. J. McGonagle Collection.

the boot to the ankle. Around the waist was a wide-banded blue plastic belt with a yellow horizontal lightning bolt on the buckle. Attached to one side of the belt was a scabbard which held **Captain Action's** silver "Lightning Sword."

Inside the box was a small color booklet showing photos of all nine of the different characters that **Captain Action** could become.

During the second and third issue, **Captain Action** figures contained a special Flasher or Videomatic ring. This premium flashed the famous pose of **Captain Action** with sword and gun and then, when turned, showed the **Captain Action** emblem.

All of the outfits were made of a stretch nylon-type fabric. The costumes were brightly colored and had various stickers and additional capes corresponding to each hero.

As for the Super Hero outfits, Ideal designers and the comic book publishers must not have communicated sufficiently about some of the heroes represented by **Captain Action**. This error was paramount in regards to **Superman**, who carried a chunk of Kryptonite in the package! **Superman** also came with **Krypto**! As any comic lover knows, **Kryp-**

One side of the color booklet found inside Captain Action boxes. J. McGonagle Collection.

to was the sidekick of **Superboy**, not **Superman**! Other irregularities included swim fins for **Aquaman** and a laser rifle for **Captain America**.

Aside from these few errors, the costumes were identical to those of the comic book-portrayed Super Heroes. The plastic boots and gloves were made of a bulky, lightweight plastic that, after long use, split at the seams much like the boots and gloves for **G. I. Joe**. The author's **Captain America** outfit had a white plastic stick-on star and white stripes which also deteriorated after much use. These are examples of why **Captain Action** items in mint condition are so collectable.

The first issue costumes included **Aquaman**, **Batman**, **Captain America**, **Flash Gordon**, **Lone Ranger**, **Phantom**, **Sgt. Fury**, **Steve Canyon**, and **Superman**.

In 1967, four new **Captain Action** costumes were offered, when **Buck Rogers**, **Green Hornet**, **Spider-man**, and **Tonto** entered the ranks of **C. A.** characters. All four new suits, as well as the re-issue of the first nine suits, came with Videomatic rings of each

character, except for **Sgt. Fury**. These rings, when tilted, showed either **Captain Action** or the character he was portraying. (A larger use of Videomatic or Flasher material is discussed in the **Mattel Secret Wars** chapter.)

There were some differences in the second issue costumes. Between 1966 and 1968, the **Phantom** costume came with two different sets of guns. The common set was a pair of six-shooters, but the scarcer set came with a pair of .45 automatics.

The **Lone Ranger** costume came in two versions. The first series **Lone Ranger** outfit came with a red shirt and black pants as depicted in early **Lone Ranger** stories from the 1930s and 1940s. The later **Lone Ranger** costumes came with a blue shirt and pants, as worn by Clayton Moore in the TV version. Both costumes came in the same type of box which depicted the **Lone Ranger** in the blue shirt.

The **Flash Gordon** costume also had an outfit change. The space suit usually came with two plug connections in the lower chest center, but some suits are reported to be without plugs.

ACTION BOY

Action Boy was introduced during the 1966-67 hype of "kid heroes." This was a time when the comic books began to create teen heroes to appeal to the younger generation. This generation gobbled up Super Heros such as **Aqualad**, **Robin**, **Speedy** (sidekick of **Green Arrow**), **Kid-Flash**, and **Superboy**. Ideal was not going to let **Captain Action** miss this bandwagon. At that time, every hero had to have a side kick.

Action Boy was issued in two different boxes and in two different costumes. For the first issue, in 1967, **Action Boy** was dressed in a red and blue outfit with a triangular **Action Boy** insignia on his chest, a blue beret on his head (with the same insignia), a silver boomerang, a yellow and silver knife, blue belt, and black boots. He was issued with a black panther, a yellow collar, and blue leash. For some reason, the panther was never given a name by Ideal, but the comic book version dubbed him "**Khem.**" The box showed a painting of **Action Boy** posed with his panther. The upper left side had pictures of the three characters he could become.

The second issue **Action Boy** was dressed in a blue and silver space outfit with the **Action Boy** insignia on the chest. He had a blue and white space helmet and silver boots, the same knife as in the first issue, and a blue and silver ray gun. The belt was the same as the first issue. This version, issued between 1967 and 1968, came with the same black panther and a comic catalogue advertising other items in the **Captain Action** line.

The costumes for the 9" **Action Boy** included **Aqualad**, **Robin**, and **Superboy**. According to some collectors, there may have been a **Kato** outfit in order for the **Green Hornet/Captain Action** figure to have a sidekick. ("**Green Hornet**" was another progenitive TV series that overlapped with "**BATMAN!**" in the 1960s. "**Green Hornet**" was a bit more serious than "**BATMAN!**" **Kato** was played by Martial Arts master **Bruce Lee**.) Apparently the **Kato** outfit was just a rumor or perhaps it was designed, but never mass-produced. As with **Captain Action**, there were major differences between the outfits designed for **Action Boy**, and those outfits worn by the comic book Super Heroes.

Action Boy most diverged from the comic book heroes in his guise as **Superboy**. While the **Superboy** costume resembled that of the character from the comic, it came with the strangest accessories thus far: a silver telepathic scrambler helmet, a yellow and blue interspace language translator, and a colorful piece of laboratory equipment. *Why?* **Superboy** needed no accessories; but, then again, accessories came with every other costume.

Four of the many outfits for Captain Action. Each box came with the outfit, a face mask (sometimes in two parts), boots and/or gloves, and accessories pertaining to the hero. NOTE: Television Batman Adam West's autograph appears on the lower-left corner of the standing Batman outfit box. J. McGonagle Collection.

DOCTOR EVIL

Dr. Evil was introduced in 1966-67 as **Captain Action's** nemesis. The 12" tall **Dr. Evil** came from Alpha Centurai complete with disguises "to hide his evil deeds" and "comes with evil outfit and evil, evil things!" He resembled a typical space alien with a blue-green skull-type head with white "bug-eyes" (an astute description). He wore a reversible satin outfit that was similar to a pair of pajamas of blue and yellow fabric. Sandals completed his **Fu Manchu**-type outfit.

The **Dr. Evil** doll came in two different boxes. The first box was basically the same as **Captain Action's** fourth issue box and had a photo of **Dr. Evil** standing over **Captain Action**. The accessories that accompanied **Dr. Evil** were a red and blue ray gun, a gold chain, and a medallion. He was first issued in 1967, but the rarer figure is of the second issue.

The second issue **Dr. Evil** box was about the same size as the uniform and equipment sets for **Captain Action**. It had a see-through cellophane display box top and inside was **Dr. Evil** on the left-hand side, and to the right was an array of various laboratory equipment, including lab shirt, hypodermic needle-type ray gun, an Evil hypnotic eye, oriental mask, mind control helmet, magnifying glass, stand for the evil

eyeball, and accessories similar to the first box. This set appeared in 1968.

CAPTAIN ACTION ACCESSORIES

QUICK-CHANGE CHAMBER and VINYL HEADQUARTERS

The Headquarters, which can be most readily found by collectors, and was thought of as the first accessory, was really the second accessory for **Captain Action**.

The first accessory, which appeared in the comic-catalogue enclosed with **Captain Action** figures, was the "Quick-Change Chamber for 1966" retailed by Sears. The catalogue advertisement was the only available material in which to reference this accessory. It was listed as a "colorful detailed cardboard transformation chamber with swinging door, sets up quickly." It was about 18" wide by 13" high and originally sold with a **Captain Action** doll, **Batman** costume, and **Captain Action/Batman** Videomatic ring — all in a gift set for $7.99.

It is not difficult to understand why **Batman's** costume was so popular. 1966 was the year of the "**BATMAN!**" TV show which made him the most popular Super Hero of the year and probably of the decade.

Dr. Evil, Captain Action's dark nemesis, is putting on one of his evil disguises!

Just about any type of item you can imagine was licensed as a **Batman** item.

This second accessory was a Sears-marketed **Captain Action** carrying case headquarters. When the case was opened, it had a small room to the left, with a green chair and computers on the wall and a small round see-through window on the far left. To the right was a clothes locker for costumes. There was also a green shelf in the locker for equipment storage. When closed, the upper part of the case read "CAPTAIN ACTION" and had a picture of **Captain Action** defending his fortress.

The case had "IDEAL TOY COMPANY" printed in the lower right-hand corner and was not dated. It was shown in the 1967 Sears Christmas catalogue and is a rare item. This item was also sold as a set with **Captain Action** doll, **Batman** costume, and Videomatic ring, all for $9.99. The case was 14" x 12" x 5" deep.

SILVER STREAK

The Silver Streak is the three-wheeled amphibian vehicle of **Captain Action**. This vehicle held two **Captain Action** figures and shot two red rockets, had a steerable front wheel, and is the rarest of items in mint condition.

By 1967, Ideal knew that it could market **Captain Action** for only one or two more years. Toy fads changed swiftly during the 1960s. The ever escalating race for the moon excited an almost unlimited merchandising potential, and space toys became among the most successful of playthings for boys. Ideal reacted by throwing everything they could into **Captain Action** to highlight Christmas of 1967. Unfortunately, their efforts did not include new costumes, although they did include new accessories for 1968.

Frequently toy manufacturers looked at the most marketable Super Heroes, rather than the most

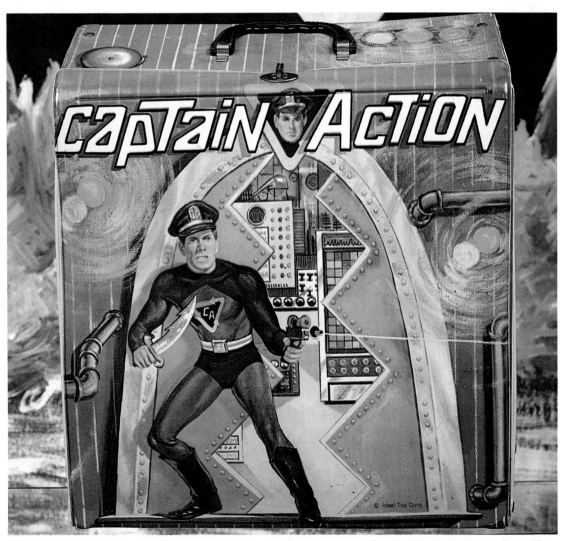

Captain Action's Vinyl Headquarters was a major accessory for 1966. J. McGonagle Collection.

Captain Action's Silver Streak. Both he and Action Boy could take this amphibious craft to any crime, on land or sea. J. McGonagle Collection.

popular or those with a loyal following, when planning toy production. Collectors agree that as children, they would have loved to have seen Super Heroes like **Thor**, **Green Arrow**, **Hulk**, **Hawkman**, or any one of the **Fantastic Four**. **Dr. Evil** could have been transformed into a great **Dr. Doom**, **Mr. Freeze**, **Dr. Octopus**, or **Bizarro**.

Collector John McGonagle gives this tidbit: "Outside sources tell me that they have seen or know of others who have seen **Captain Action** outfits of everything from the original **Captain Marvel (SHAZAM!)** and **Tom Corbett** to **Dr. Evil** costumes of the **Joker**, **Green Goblin**, and the **Penguin**. Still others tell us that Ideal made a **Captain Action** Batmobile. In the twelve years I have collected **Captain Action** memorabilia, and having purchased most of the toys by the early 1970s, I have never seen these items!"

ACTION CAVE

Montgomery Ward, not to be outdone by Sears, sold the **Captain Action** Action Cave carrying case for Christmas of 1967. This item started out as a Batcave for a 1966 **Batman** playset, but in 1967 Wards switched it to the then-popular **Captain Action**. The carrying case was shaped like an "M" or a mountain, depending on how you looked at it.

The outside lithography showed **Captain Action**, **Action Boy**, and **Khem** the panther defending their mountainside fortress. It was very colorful and would have made another great headquarters for **Captain Action**, if not for its size. It was originally made for three-inch figures and the insides looked like the Batcave. Unfortunately, unlike Mego toys, there were no three-inch figures of **Captain Action**. When opened, it only stood about ten inches high by fifteen inches wide and three to four inches deep. Regardless of its unusually small size, it is a very rare **Captain Action** collectible, especially in mint condition.

CAPTAIN ACTION/DR. EVIL MOUNTAINTOP SANCTUARY

The **Dr. Evil/Captain Action** Mountaintop Sanctuary of 1967-68 was described in the 1967 Ideal toy catalogue as a "Space-Age carrying case, with storage bins for outfits and accessories."

This accessory was widely available in most toy stores that carried **Captain Action** toys. In the catalogue, **Dr. Evil** was depicted occupying the swivel cockpit, surrounded by a realistically-illustrated crime laboratory, while he spied on his enemy through a see-through window. On the craggy exterior were famous comic heroes plus **Action Boy** and **Dr. Evil**. About fifteen inches high, it was made of vinyl-covered cardboard. Despite the wide retailing of this accessory, it is a hard item to find.

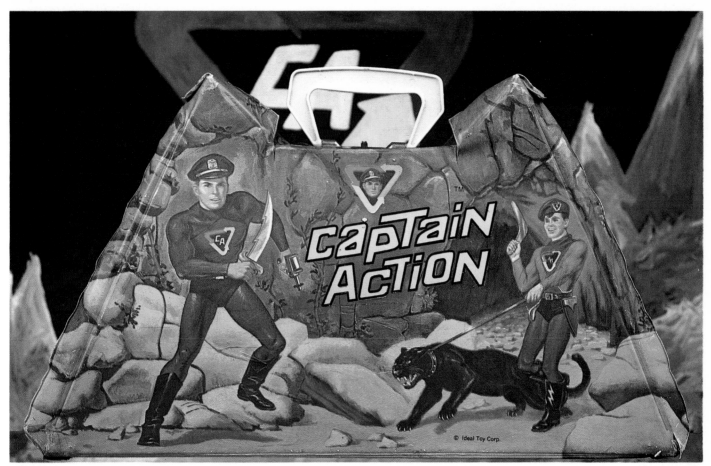

Captain Action's Action Cave. Captain Action is seen here with Action Boy, preparing to battle evil. J. McGonagle Collection.

CAPTAIN ACTION GARAGE/HIDEOUT

Sears also retailed the Silver Streak Garage/Headquarters in 1967. Sears claimed that "Only Sears included a fortified garage with **Captain Action's** Silver Streak Car." All that is presently known about this item is that it was big enough to hold the 21-inch Silver Streak Car.

SMALLER ACCESSORIES

If large accessories were not enough, there were a few sets of smaller ones. They included:

**INTER-SPACIAL DIRECTIONAL
    COMMUNICATOR**

SURVIVAL KIT

WEAPONS ARSENAL

ANTI-GRAVITATIONAL POWER PACK

INTER-GALACTIC JET MORTAR

FOUR FOOT WORKING PARACHUTE (The parachute was a re-issue of the same parachute given away with the second series **Captain Action** doll. Silver boots and orange helmet were added to this set.)

OTHER FACTS

It is interesting to note that Aurora made a model kit of **Captain Action** in 1965. The model depicted **Captain Action** in his famous pose and when built stood fifteen inches tall or 1/5th scale. The model is highly valued by **Captain Action** collectors.

Captain Action was a first in comic book/toy history. Collectors seem to concur that **Captain Action** was the first **Super Hero** to be a toy and then a comic book hero. It was not until the 1970s and the likes of the **Micronauts**, **He-Man**, **Mask**, and the 1980s **G.I. Joe** and **Thundercats** that this switch of the toy to comic book idea occurred again.

Captain Action's comic book debut was less than popular. Only five issues of the series were published before DC Comics (then National Periodicals) canceled it.

The first issue cover showed **Captain Action**, **Action Boy**, and the panther pushing **Superman** out of the way, exclaiming, "This is a job for **Captain Action** and Company." Most, if not all, of the artwork was done by the team of Gil Kane and Wally Wood. The story was written by Jim Shooter, who was later Editor-in-Chief of Marvel Comics.

Only Sears includes a fortified garage with Captain Action's Silver Streak Car

$7⁹⁹

Captain Action, Action Boy not included

Runs on land and floats in water to help Captain Action defend both the land and sea. Sleek twin seater is custom made for he and Action Boy. Spring operated turbo rockets actually fire. Tri wheel design. Removable deck, radar scanner. Plastic. 21 inches long. Stores in cardboard garage. 79 N 5937C Wt 3 lbs $7.99

The small comic-catalogues that came with the various outfits were drawn by Chick Stone.

A very un-final note to the legend of **Captain Action**: rumor had it that **Captain Action** was to appear in a new comic series initially scheduled to premier in late 1987; in September 1988 we are still waiting.

IDEAL SUPER QUEEN SERIES

The Ideal "Super Queen" series of female Super Heroes was made for the girls of the 1960s. Most **Captain Action** collectors consider these figures an important part of their collections because the dolls were scaled to the **Captain Action** figure and they are the female counterparts of the Super Heroes characterized by **Captain Action**!

Each one had the traditional outfit for the female character and a set of accessories; three of the heroines also came with halter dresses for their secret identities. Only **Mera**, wife of **Aquaman**, came without an extra dress, since she had no alter ego! The other three heroines included **Batgirl** (a.k.a. **Barbara Gordon**), **Supergirl** (a.k.a. **Linda Lee Danvers**), and **Wonder Woman** (a.k.a. **Diana Prince**).

KNIGHT OF DARKNESS
Captain Action revisited!

Just when you thought it was safe to finish your collection, along came the **Knight of Darkness**. This doll was produced in 1978 and was garbed to rival Kenner's **Star Wars** toy line.

Ideal used a few old characters to make up its line of five new figures of various sizes, but none other than **Captain Action** was re-used for the **Knight of Darkness** figure. This 12" figure was dressed in a black and silver suit, black cape, and black boots. Now for the best part: except for his vinyl black and

silver robot-like head, this figure was a jet-black dyed **Captain Action**!

Yes, the same body mold! If that was not enough, the **Knight's** ray gun was the same as that which came with **Captain Action's Flash Gordon** outfit, and the black boots were **Captain Action's** boots, complete with lightning bolt!

The **Knight of Darkness** can be an interesting find for any collector, but if you do come across one, be careful. The black dye was very poorly applied and will leave a dark purple stain on anything it touches.

Now back to **Captain Action**...

LISTINGS

FIRST and FOURTH ISSUE CAPTAIN ACTION: Blue and black uniform with the triangular red, green, and yellow **Captain Action** logo in the center; blue combination cap with an anchor centered over the silver-braided brim; black plastic boots with horizontal lightning bolts stretching from the pointed top of the boot to the ankle; around the waist was a wide-banded blue plastic belt with a yellow horizontal lightning bolt on the buckle; attached to one side of the belt was a scabbard which held the silver "Lightning Sword."

SECOND ISSUE CAPTAIN ACTION: Identical to above, but showed the blue **Lone Ranger** shirt.

Wonder Woman, one of the Ideal Super Queens, is shown in her box beside an un-boxed Batgirl. J. McGonagle Collection.

Action Boy was Captain Action's 1967 partner in crime-fighting. Here we see both issues of Action Boy and the second issue Action Boy box. J. McGonagle Collection.

THIRD ISSUE CAPTAIN ACTION: Identical to above, but box contained a special Flasher or Videomatic ring and parachute.

Values are for Good and Excellent.

First Issue (Late 1966):	**200**	**300**
Second Issue (Christmas 1966):	**200**	**350**
Third Issue (Early 1967):	**300**	**400**
Fourth Issue (Christmas 1967):	**250**	**400**

FIRST ISSUE ACTION BOY: Dressed in a red and blue outfit with a triangular **Action Boy** insignia on his chest, a blue beret on his head (with the same insignia), a silver boomerang, a yellow and silver knife, blue belt, and black boots. He was accompanied by **Khem,** the black panther, who had a yellow collar and blue leash.

SECOND ISSUE ACTION BOY: Dressed in a blue and silver space outfit with the **Action Boy** insignia on the chest. He had a blue and white space helmet and silver boots, the same knife as in the first issue, and a blue and silver ray gun. The belt was the same as the first issue. This version, issued between 1967 and 1968, also came with the same black panther. The doll came with a comic catalogue showing the other items in the **Captain Action** line.

First Issue:	**275**	**375**
Second Issue:	**325**	**495**

FIRST ISSUE DR. EVIL: Blue-green skull-type head with white bulging eyes; he wore a reversible satin outfit that resembled a pair of blue and yellow pajamas; blue sandals. The first issue box resembled **Captain Action's** fourth issue box and had a photo of **Dr. Evil** standing over **Captain Action.** The accessories that came with **Dr. Evil** were a red and blue ray gun, a gold chain, and a medallion. He was first issued in 1967, but the rarer boxed figure was of the second issue in 1968.

SECOND ISSUE DR. EVIL: Box was about the same size as the uniform and equipment sets for **Captain Action.** It had a see-through cellophane display box top and inside was **Dr. Evil** on the left-hand side, and to the right was an array of various laboratory equipment, including lab shirt, hypodermic needle-type ray gun, an Evil hypnotic eye, oriental mask, mind control helmet, magnifying glass, stand for evil eyeball, and accessories similar to the first box. This set appeared in 1968.

First Issue:	**275**	**375**
Second Issue:	**325**	**475**

CAPTAIN ACTION OUTFITS

All outfits were made of nylon-type fabric with plastic masks and various accessories. **NOTE:** John McGonagle notes that the lip color on all of the masks may vary from

G. I. Joe disguised as Aquaman, Bulletman (an unknown action figure) disguised as Superman, and Captain Action diguised as Batman. NOTE: Krypto the Superdog is to the right of Superman. J. McGonagle Collection.

orange to bright red or from pink to white. In some cases the lips were dark on the outside and white in the middle to illustrate teeth.

AQUAMAN: 1966; **Aquaman** face mask with blonde hair and eyebrows, mouth open; traditional outfit except with yellow fins with green trim; accessories included yellow spear with silver trident tip, pink conch horn, swordfish sword, and knife with sheath.   **115   195**

AQUAMAN: 1967; identical to above, but with Videomatic ring.   **145   245**

BATMAN: 1966; **Batman** two-piece face mask with cowl, blue cape with black stripes, gray and blue body suit with gold and black Batsymbol, blue boots, blue and silver Bat utility belt with loops to hold accessories, blue and silver Bat flashlight, blue and silver Bat drill, Bat grappling hook with cord on reel, and blue Batarang.   **115   175**

BATMAN: 1967; identical to above, but with Videomatic ring.   **145   175**

BUCK ROGERS: 1967; one-piece face mask with light brown hair and eyebrows, metallic blue helmet (resembled a Roman Gladiator helmet), silver suit with decals, red vinyl reversible vest with black trim, black pointed boots, black rubber gloves, black and yellow belt and harness with silver trim; radio microphone with cord attached to belt, two "heat-sensing" metallic blue rockets with yellow tips, silver canteen, and silver flashlight; with Videomatic ring.   **200   300**

CAPTAIN AMERICA: 1966; **Captain America** face mask with open mouth; traditional outfit, star and white stripes were stickers; accessories included belt with holster and ultrasonic pistol, laser beam gun, removable boots and gloves, and traditional round shield.

115   195

CAPTAIN AMERICA: 1967; identical to above, but with Videomatic ring.   **145   225**

FLASH GORDON: 1966; face mask with white/blonde hair and eyebrows, smiling lips; very untraditional outfit shown as a silver astronaut-type suit; accessories included space helmet; space belt with holster, and ray pistol plus attached ALGAE (Activated Atmospheric Balance Generator), guidance gun, compressed oxygen tank, and removable silver boots, plugs on suit.   **115   195**

FLASH GORDON: 1967; identical to above, but with Videomatic ring.   **145   225**

FLASH GORDON: 1967; identical to above, but without plugs on suit.   **145   225**

GREEN HORNET: 1967; **Green Hornet** one-piece flesh-colored face with green mask; black fedora with green band; white scarf; green overcoat with black felt buttons, collar, and pockets; black pants, socks, and loafer-style shoes; green shoulder holster and gas gun; yellow gas mask, black hornet sting; gold and white pocket watch radio and large black and silver TV communications device; and Videomatic ring.   **275   500**

NOTE: *In a recent* **Captain Action** *auction, a* **Green Hornet***, in mint condition, was sold for over $2,500!*

LONE RANGER: 1966; **Lone Ranger** face mask with Type 2B mask; black trousers with blue leather-trimmed shirt; accessories included gun belt with two holsters and two pistols, boots with spurs, Winchester rifle, and white cowboy hat.   **115   195**

LONE RANGER: 1967; identical to above, with two-piece blue outfit.   **145   225**

PHANTOM: 1966; **Phantom** face mask with open mouth; traditional outfit; accessories included rifle with scope, belt with twin holsters and six-shooter-type pistols, knife, and removable boots.   **115   195**

PHANTOM: 1967; identical to above, but with Videomatic ring.   **145   225**

PHANTOM: 1967; identical to above, but with .45 automatics.   **145   225**

SGT. FURY: 1966; **Sgt. Fury** face mask with closed mouth and five o' clock shadow; camouflage Army attire; accessories included helmet with chin strap, gun belt with

Captain Action (center) is flanked by the Phantom (left) and Captain America (right). Note that the Phantom is actually G. I. Joe in disguise! J. McGonagle and J. Makowski Collections.

Captain Action and G. I. Joe disguised as Spider-Man, the Lone Ranger (in blue), and the Green Hornet. J. McGonagle Collection.

.45 automatic and holster, walkie-talkie, bandolier, three hand grenades, machine gun, and removable plastic combat boots.   **115   195**

SPIDER-MAN: 1967; **Spider-Man** one-piece face mask with cut-out eyes and black trim; red, blue, and black traditional body suit, red boots; accessories included red web sword, silver and red web fluid tank, black spider grappling hook, silver flashlight, and red belt to hold accessories.   **275   450**

STEVE CANYON: 1966; face mask with open mouth and yellow hair with black stripe to represent part in hair; olive green paratrooper's uniform; accessories included 50-mission hat, parachute pack, garrison belt with holster and .45 automatic revolver, helmet with oxygen mask, and removable flight boots.   **115   195**

STEVE CANYON: 1967; identical to above, but with Videomatic ring.   **145   225**

SUPERMAN: 1966; **Superman** face mask (complete with cowlick); traditional outfit; accessories included arm

shackles, block of green Kryptonite, removable boots, and **Krypto the Superdog** with cape.   **115   175**

SUPERMAN: 1967; identical to above, but with Videomatic ring.   **145   225**

TONTO: 1967; **Tonto** one-piece face mask, one piece headband with feather; brown two-piece suit pants and shirt with fringe, brown with yellow fringe; gun belt with holster and scabbard, well-detailed moccasins; brown and black indian bow, brown and black quiver, four arrows with red, blue, yellow, and green feathers, black and silver six-gun, silver knife with black handle, and **Taka**, eagle sidekick.   **200   300**

ACTION BOY OUTFITS

All outfits made of nylon-type fabric with plastic masks and various accessories.

AQUALAD: 1967; one-piece face mask with black hair and eye trim, and orange lips; body suit made up of red shirt, blue trunks; flesh-colored legs, blue boots, black belt with yellow "A" buckle; green-trimmed knife scabbard and hook to hold axe, red and gray sea shell axe, silver and yellow swordfish spear, silver and yellow sea horse knife. Came with green pet octopus, **Octo.**   **150   300**

ROBIN: 1967; one-piece face mask with black hair, mask over eyes, red lips; detailed body suit in red, green, and black with gold trim; yellow plastic cape with buckle; short green boots; small green rubber gloves; black belt with yellow buckle and loops to hold accessories; large green and black Batarang launcher, two red Batarangs, blue and red Bat grenade, two blue and gold climbing grips.   **175   350**

SUPERBOY: 1967; one-piece face mask with black hair, light red lips and cowlick; body suit was traditional blue with red trunks and gold/red "S" emblem; attached red plastic cape; red boots; yellow belt with "S" on buckle; silver telepathic scrambler helmet, yellow and blue inter-

space language translator, and colorful chemical laboratory piece.   **175   350**

CAPTAIN ACTION ACCESSORY SETS

ANTI-GRAVITATIONAL POWER PACK: 1967; included blue jet pack with chrome trim, silver helmet (resembles race car driver's helmet), silver gloves, silver boots, and belt to hold jet pack.   **95   175**

INTER-GALACTIC JET MORTAR: 1967; included shoulder actionmatic blaster, blaster tripod, radar scanner dish, and ammunition carrier with two red nuclear warhead missiles.   **95   175**

INTER-SPACIAL DIRECTIONAL COMMUNICATOR: 1967; included solar-energized power pack, rotating antennae dome, anti-static power plug, hand-held signal beam projector, and secret frequency sound horn.   **95   175**

Action Boy (left) stands next to (left to right) Robin, Superboy, and Aqualad. Note the accessories and Octo the octopus in foreground. J. McGonagle and J. Makowski Collections.

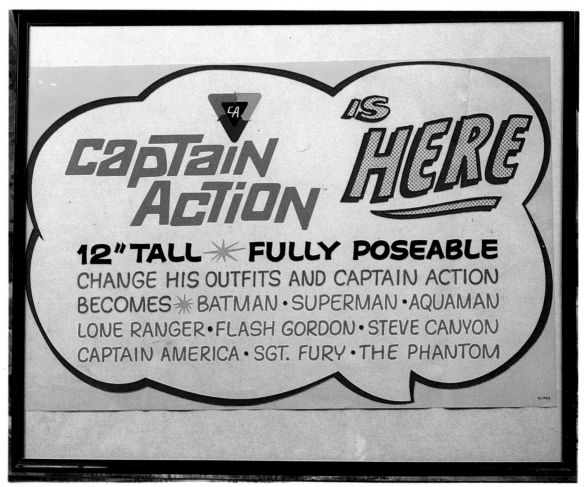

This Captain Action sales poster is one of the rarest of Captain Action collectibles. J. Makowski Collection.

SURVIVAL KIT: 1967; included first aid kit, mirror, utility belt with one-piece molded action rope, dagger/switchblade, hatchet, flare pistols, RWB flares, and ammo box; orange two-piece vest, folding spade, machete, three-piece extension claw, emergency fishing kit, and high frequency radio.   95   175

WEAPONS ARSENAL: 1967; included weapons rack, laser rifle, ray pistol, two .45 automatics, machine gun, six-shooter, two different kinds of knives, and two hand grenades.   95   175

FOUR-FOOT WORKING PARACHUTE: 1967; blue vinyl parachute packs into orange harness, orange football-type helmet, and silver boots.   75   100

Large Accessories

ACTION CAVE: Carrying case is 10" tall by 15" wide and 3" to 4" deep; illustrated on outside with **Captain Action, Action Boy,** and pet panther; inside illustrations resemble Batcave.   375   650

CAPTAIN ACTION/DR. EVIL SANCTUARY: 15" high in vinyl-covered cardboard; exterior had illustration of famous comic heroes, **Action Boy** and **Dr. Evil;** inside in-cluded storage bins, swivel cockpit, and see-through window; inside illustrations showed laboratory.   **NRS**

GARAGE/HIDEOUT: 21" deep; other information unknown.   **NRS**

QUICK CHANGE CHAMBER: Colorfully detailed cardboard set up; 18" high by 13" wide with swinging door. Originally came with **Captain Action** doll, **Batman** costume, and **Captain Action/Batman** Videomatic ring. Other details unknown.   **NRS**

SILVER STREAK AMPHIBIAN CAR: 20" long; three-wheeled light blue amphibian vehicle; seated two figures; shot two red rockets which were included; steerable front wheel rod in cockpit. Many detailed decorations inside, and outside of cockpit.   350   600

VINYL HEADQUARTERS: 14" high by 12" wide and 5" deep; vinyl carrying case had rooms on the inside. Left room had a green plastic chair and computers on wall with small round window on far left; right room had a clothes locker and small green shelf; outside of case had illustrations of **Captain Action** and labels "CAPTAIN ACTION" and "IDEAL TOY COMPANY". Originally came with **Cap-**

tain **Action** doll, **Batman** costume, and **Captain Action/Batman** Videomatic ring.   **400** **595**

Box Accessories

PHOTO-CATALOGUE: First Issue.   **10** **25**

COMIC-CATALOGUE: Second Issue.   **15** **45**

VIDEOMATIC RING.   **5** **20**

SUPER QUEENS

It is not known how many differently-colored halter dresses there were or if there was a method to tell which color went with which costume.

BATGIRL: 1967; black body suit with gold and black Batsymbol, blue vinyl cowl, blue plastic cape, blue boots, gold belt with gold and black Batsymbol, and blue Batarang; **Barbara Gordon** halter dress.   **95** **300**

MERA: 1967; green and yellow body suit, belt, yellow crown, and yellow and silver trident.   **90** **295**

SUPERGIRL: 1967; blue skirt and blouse with traditional **Superman** symbol, gold belt, red plastic cape, red boots; **Krypto the Superdog** and **Linda Lee Danvers** halter dress.   **95** **300**

WONDER WOMAN: 1967; red and blue top and shorts with gold chest emblem, belt, red plastic high-heeled strap boots, golden tiara, golden lasso, and **Diana Prince** halter dress.   **95** **300**

KNIGHT OF DARKNESS

1984; 12" tall; black and silver robot-like head; dressed in a black and silver suit, black cape, black boots; and ray gun.   **10** **35**

In addition to the amazing success of Ideal's Captain Action, the company produced a series of three-inch Super Heroes called the Ideal "Justice League" figures. Shown here (left to right) are Superman, Robin, Batman, Joker, Flash, Aquaman, and Wonder Woman. All but Joker came in both painted and unpainted sets; the Joker shown here was painted by John McGonagle's mother. Behind the painted figures are the boxed unpainted figures of Robin, Batman, and Joker. Beside the box are the unpainted figures of Koltar and Keyman. J. McGonagle Collection.

NOTE: *The marketing success of Ideal's* **Captain Action** *made headlines in the toy world that rivaled Hasbro's* **G. I. Joe**. *Just as sales of* **Captain Action** *began to climb, Ideal presented the* **Justice League** *figures. Though not true action figures according to our definition, these figures warrant our attention.*

The three-inch Super Heroes were each hand-painted and resembled the smallest scale models instead of toys; but, they were just highly-detailed plastic soldiers.

John McGonagle, a fanatical collector, has prepared the following article on these small figures.

THE JUSTICE LEAGUE FIGURES
Ideal's Number Two Super Heroes
By John McGonagle

This set, consisting of six Super Heroes, included **Batman**, **Superman**, **Robin** (although **Robin** was never a member of the comic book **Justice League of America** or **JLA**), **Flash**, **Aquaman**, and **Wonder Woman**. For the most part, they were sold in four-packs, each with two heroes and two villains.

The Bad Guys included **Joker**, **Brainstorm**, **Keyman**, **Koltar**, **Thunderbolt**, and **Mouseman**. Originally, **Thunderbolt**, a.k.a. **Johnny Thunder**, the **Human Thunderbolt**, was a good guy in the com-

ics, but the folks at Ideal apparently thought he made a much better villain!

The bad guys were not hand-painted but were highly detailed and molded in bright colors. It is possible to tell if you have found either a hero or a villain by looking at the bottom of the base for the name of the figure, and company, and the year in Roman numerals.

The four-packs included decorated blister packs with colorful illustrations on the background cards.

6-Piece Batman and Robin Set
. . includes Bat-Car, Gotham City

Only at Sears $1.89

23-piece Batman and Robin Set

With Bat-Car, Bat-Plane and other accessories for fast action that foils 6 villains . . you even get a Sanctuary Mountain $4.99 set

This page from the 1967 Sears Wish Book shows the entire Justice League figure set offered that year.

The Joker figure has never been found factory-painted. S. Kimball Collection.

Ideal also manufactured three special figures as a set, namely, **Batman**, **Robin**, and the **Joker**. These figures were also not hand-painted but came in different molded plastic colors: **Batman** in gray, **Robin** in yellow, and the **Joker** in blue. This set was called the "Official **Batman** Figure Set."

Also, Ideal made two special sets for Sears during 1966-67; the first set, according to the catalogue, was made for the "Pee Wee Bat Fan." This set included figures of **Batman**, **Robin**, and two villains, plastic seven-inch Batmobile, and an exciting-looking 9" x 15" Gothem City background made of colorful cardboard.

The second set had 23 pieces, and included the same figures as the first set with the addition of a Batplane, six villains, a deadly robot figure, red plastic Bat Signal, plastic machines and buildings, and a hard plastic mountain sanctuary and the Bat Cave. The six-piece set was much rarer than the large 23-piece set.

Ideal obviously made more of the **Batman** related figures because of the TV Show, but some fellow collectors believe that Ideal made a **Justice League of America** playset, with all 12 figures in one package. If any reader has such a set, please let us know.

LISTINGS

BASIC FOUR-PACK: Blister packs included two heroes and two villains (assorted). **50   145**

BATMAN THREE-PACK: Blister packs included **Batman**, **Robin**, and **Joker**. **15   35**

SEARS SIX-PACK: Very rare, few details known.

NRS

SEARS 23-PIECE BATMAN PLAYSET: Included **Batman**, **Robin**, six assorted villains, robot, Batmobile, Batplane, red Batsignal, plastic machines and buildings, a hard plastic mountain sanctuary, and Bat Cave.

100   275

SINGLE PAINTED FIGURES: Various.   **5   25**

SINGLE UNPAINTED FIGURES: Various.   **2   15**

SIX UNPAINTED VILLAINS: Various.   **5   20**

JUSTICE LEAGUE OF AMERICA PLAYSET: No details known.   **NRS**

In this photograph we see a few of the Marx plastic army soldier-type figures of the 1960s. Though these are not considered action figures, they are still listed because they make up one of the very few attempts by Marx at producing Super Hero figures. From left to right are Thor, Captain America, Iron Man, and the Hulk. J. McGonagle Collection.

MISCELLANEOUS 1960s FIGURES

To include some of the "off-the-wall" or less important singular figures, we have decided to list these figures at the end of this chapter. The following figures may not represent action figures, but are of interest to Super Hero action figure collectors. We would like to thank **Hake's Americana & Collectibles** for assisting with descriptions and photographs.

LISTINGS

SUPERMAN PUSH BUTTON TOY (KOHNER BROTHERS): 1966; 5-1/4" tall jointed plastic toy on 2" x 2" base; Jointed **Superman** figure in traditional uniform colors. When push button underneath the base was pushed, **Superman** collapsed forward, backward, or to the sides. Made in Hong Kong. Courtesy Hake's Americana & Collectibles.   **15   25**

ROBIN (IDEAL): 1966; 3-1/4" tall fully-dimensional painted plastic figure on base; made in Portugal. We would like readers who have these figures or have photographs of these figures to verify how many types were made. Courtesy Hake's Americana & Collectibles.   **10   15**

THE ORIGINAL, ACTION-PACKED SWINGING... (FUN THINGS): 1966; 6" rubber figure on a string with plastic loop at the end.

(A) **Batman**.	**10**	**15**
(B) **Robin**.	**10**	**15**
(C) **Superman**.	**10**	**15**

MECHANICAL SUPER HEROES (MARX): 1968; 3-1/2" x 3-1/2" x 5-1/2" tall windup tin figures.

(A) **Captain America**.	**40**	**60**
(B) **Spider-Man**.	**40**	**60**
(C) **Superman**.	**40**	**60**
(D) **Batman**.	**40**	**60**

The Superman Push Button Toy, while not an action figure, is articulated at various anatomical points. Push Button Toys will be described in later volumes of Greenberg's Guide to Super Hero Toys. Photo courtesy of Hake's Americana & Collectibles.

MARX PLASTIC MARVEL SUPER HEROES SET: 1967; toy soldier-sized plastic figures on base.

Set:	25	50
(A) **Captain America.**	5	10
(B) **Spider-Man.**	5	10
(C) **Thor.**	5	10
(D) **Daredevil.**	5	10
(E) **Iron Man.**	5	10
(F) **Hulk.**	5	10

Note: These figures may have been used again in the mid-1970s. See the Miscellaneous Listings for the 1970s.

BATMAN MARIONETTE: 1960s; 14-1/2" tall marionette with painted composition head and hands with fabric clothing. He had a purple cape resembling **Batman's**, but the rest of his outfit was a dark blue sweater with black sleeves and dark pink trousers. His mask was light blue and the bottom of his face and hands were pink flesh tone. His feet were a yellow-orange wood and Mexico was stamped on the bottom. Courtesy Hake's Americana & Collectibles.   **50   100**

FLYING SUPERMAN (HASBRO): 1965; fully-dimensional figure was solid blue molded plastic; his cape was a piece of formed dark pink styrofoam; the two pieces were held together by rubber band strapping and there was also a 6" wood launching rod to propel the figure by means of a rubber band slingshot-like arrangement. Detailed display card. Courtesy Hake's Americana & Collectibles.   **30   60**

"IMPISH" ROBIN: c. 1960-70s; 5-1/2" tall hollow soft vinyl figure of imp-like **Robin** with tiny freckles and one front tooth. He had artificial black hair and his outfit was mostly traditional. Mask and cape were made of felt. Made in Japan. Courtesy Hake's Americana & Collectibles.   **30   60**

One of the most popular of the inexpensive Super Hero toys of the 1960s, Fun Things' action-packed swinging Superman was suitable for your rear view mirror. S. Kimball Collection.

NOTE: There are obviously many toy action figures that were made in small numbers. In future editions of this book, we hope to list them all. Please fill in the correction/addition form attached to the inside front cover to help us in this ongoing research.

Atom Ant and Secret Squirrel, represented here by their push-up counterparts, shared a successful Saturday morning cartoon program during the mid-1960s. It was revived during the 1970s for daily after school viewing. Nowadays, one can find repeats of these and other Hanna-Barbera cartoons on the Cartoon Express, Turner Broadcasting's USA Network cable channel. J. Armacost Collection.

"UP AND AT 'EM ATOM ANT!"

A Look at Hanna-Barbera Super Heroes

Who can forget the Saturday morning cartoons of the late 1960s? I remember sitting in front of what my father referred to as the "idiot box," with a bowl of Honeycombs in my lap, watching a red ant in a white racing helmet flash out of a hole in the ground, leaving his mailbox shivering.

Atom Ant was just one of a few of the Hanna-Barbera Super Heroes. From 1965 to 1967 the **"Atom Ant/Secret Squirrel"** cartoon program delighted youngsters all over America with their zany cartoons. Some other cartoon favorites of mine were **"The Impossibles,"** featuring **Coil Man**, **Multi Man**, and **Fluid Man**, who were really a cross between Super Heroes and the Beatles; and the 30-foot robot

Frankenstein, Jr. with his operator/friend **Buzz Conroy**. This show's theme represented a ploy used numerous times in children's television: big robot, little boy. A similar hit of the early 1960s was **"Gigantor,"** and still another was **"Johnny Sokko and his Flying Robot"**; both programs featured large robots with child operators.

"Spaaaacce Ghooooooost!"

With that cry and a yellow sheet tied to my back, I'd "zoom" around the living room, knocking items from the coffee table to the floor. **Space Ghost**, who appeared on Saturday morning TV from 1966 to

1967, was an instant success. With **Laugh-In** announcer Gary Owens as the voice of **Space Ghost**, the show seemed better to me than all the other Hanna-Barbera cartoons. With sidekicks **Jan, Jase,** and pet monkey, **Blip, Space Ghost** rocketed throughout space in his infamous "Phantom Cruiser."

Unfortunately, I have never discovered any **Space Ghost** toys. In fact, the only item that came close to a **Space Ghost**-related toy was a cut-out-and-assemble Phantom Cruiser that I built from the back of an empty box of Post Raisin Bran in 1967.

With **Space Ghost** came an avalanche of other Super Heroes. Most were the yet-unknown creations of Hanna-Barbera. Only Marvel Comics' **Fantastic Four** were known comic book heroes. Later, Hanna-Barbera produced its own line of comic books based on their Super Hero creations.

Others shows from Hanna-Barbera included **"Young Samson and Goliath," "Galaxy Trio," "Birdman and Avenger," "Shazzan," "Moby Dick,"**

"Mighty Mightor," and another of my favorites, **"The Herculoids."**

The Herculoids were a family of cave people who befriended various weird inhabitants of the alien world in which they were all castaway. The family included **King Zandor**, his wife, **Tara**, and their son, **Dorno**. The friendly aliens were very strange. **Zok** was a flying dragon with laser beam eyes, **Igoo** was a large ape made of rock, and **Tundro** was a ten-legged Triceritops with an armadillo back who shot lava from his tusks. Finally, there was **Gloop** and **Gleep** who were glow-in-the-dark formless blobs with big black eyes.

It was not until the mid-1970s that Hanna-Barbera again brought new Super Heroes to the television screen. After the success of **Scooby-Doo** and his ilk, the company made **Dyno-Mutt**, the **Scooby-Doo** robot clone.

With **Dyno-Mutt** came the **Blue Falcon**, an underrated Super Hero, and **Captain Caveman**, who was billed as the world's first Super Hero. But who could

A plush Hong Kong Phooey and his sidekick Spot, made by the Presents division of Tomy Toys. S. Kimball Collection.

forget the voice of Scatman Cruthers as the incompetent Oriental dog-hero, **Hong Kong Phooey**.

In the accompanying picture, are some recently manufactured Super Hero plush dolls. **Secret Squirrel**, **Hong Kong Phooey**, and the like may make a comeback soon.

One place to meet Hanna-Barbera characters face to face is at **King's Dominion** amusement park in Richmond, Virginia. The author has seen many Hanna-Barbera Super Hero and other collectibles for sale there.

TERRYTOON SUPER HEROES

"It's just little ol' me,
Underdog."

Underdog is yet another hero who, like Hanna-Barbera's **Space Ghost** and **Jonny Quest**, has been recycled. The very likable Wally Cox provided the voice of **Underdog** in the 1960s, and it was this voice that brought the canine eater of Power Pills to life. Spotlight Comics is revamping this die-hard character into one of the best children's-type comic books I have ever read. This refreshing look at an old character is one of the few written *for* children without sacrificing story depth.

But the 1960s **Underdog** was incredible. Here was a hero who, in every sense of the word, reflected his title... **Underdog**. He started off on the wrong track, took the long way around, barely won a fight, and rejected poor **Polly Purebread** because of his awesome responsibility. From humble **Shoeshine Boy** to Super Hero, he was everybody's dream come true.

Another Terrytoons hero was **Batfink**. Yep, **Batfink**. Here we had an actual bat-hero who was not a man but a bat, and a large bat at that! His favorite battle cry was "My wings are like a shield of steel" as various machine-gun bullets ricocheted off of his wings with echoing twings. His sidekick, **Kato**, had neither an original name nor actions.

The **Mighty Heroes**, yet another Terrytoons group of heroes, included **Diaperman**, **Cuckooman**, **Tor-**

The Dyno-Mutt World Champion Sky-Diver figure made by the Imperial Toy Company in 1977. S. Kimball Collection.

nadoman, **Strongman**, and **Ropeman**. An "H" for Hero appeared on the chest of all the costumes except for the bare-chested **Diaperman** who wore only a diaper, baby pin, and cape! Terrytoons was probably best known for its incredible hero, **Mighty Mouse**. With an operatic "Here I come to save the day!" this small yet powerful rodent became a mainstay of the Super Hero cartoon diet. Not withstanding their popularity, no action figures have surfaced from this vast melting pot of characters.

THE 1970s

An interesting time for the Super Hero

Some of the toys manufactured and sold during the 1970s were easily broken. When you find a Mego action figure, for example, seven out of ten are broken at the forearm or knee. Surprisingly, even figures of the last Mego series arrive broken *in* the untouched blister pack! On the other hand, Mego figures found in first issue boxes are in much, much better condition. This shows the soundness of quality packaging.

In the first half of the 1970s Super Hero fandom declined. The Bat-Fad had died, and Super Heroes were left to Saturday morning programming. At first there were many Super Heroes who appeared in a blaze of hype and then disappeared within a year.

The 1970s Saturday morning line-up included **Captain Caveman** (billed as the world's first Super Hero: a caveman) and the **Blue Falcon** and **Dyno-Mutt. Blue Falcon** was a hero who could have appealed to older children if not for the cutting humor of his robot dog, **Dyno-Mutt. Dyno-Mutt** was a cross between **Scooby-Doo** and **Inspector Gadget**!

In the early 1970s, the Beatles had only recently broken up, and Super Heroes, for some reason, were suddenly in demand. Every evening, in every living room, a new and horrible violence appeared on the news programs, and it was beginning to creep into "prime-time" entertainment television shows. The range of psychology books written during that era, along with announcements by Dr. Benjamin Spock and other child psychologists concerning the Vietnam War and its violent effects on children, seemed to prompt a renewed desire for the idealistic Super Hero. People were looking for role models, and not finding them, turned to the heroes of former times. Super Heroes entered the world again.

Saturday mornings and after school evenings presented rediscovered viewing times for old Super Heroes, as well as for many new ones. Many were delighted with **"Super Friends,"** a Saturday morning event that was unparalleled in the history of "Saturday Morning Super Stars." The **Super Friends** evolved out of the animation studios of Hanna-Barbera, which held Saturday morning TV programming in the palm of its hand. For more information on Hanna-Barbera, see the Hanna-Barbera chapter.

The **Super Friends** were actually a version of DC Comics' own **Justice League of America** with a few new heroes thrown in. Each episode featured new and old villains and each story came with a moral and two short segments featuring a magic trick (performed by your favorite Super Hero) and a health tip. This was perfectly suited to both child and parent. It also launched a revitalized licensing and merchandising campaign for both DC and Marvel.

At the same time, some live action heroes came to the screen. Both **"SHAZAM!"** (**Captain Marvel**) and **"ISIS"** appeared on Saturday mornings and became hit TV shows. Later in the decade, **"The Incredible Hulk"** arrived. The show was as adventurous as it was tender, and it was by far was the best TV series to present a serious Super Hero as a star.

The **Incredible Hulk** was later the star of a Saturday morning cartoon along with the **Amazing Spider-Man**, who was also made into a live-action TV show. Unfortunately, the public did not believe in a

The inflatable Hulk is deflated. After the air bag is pumped (not shown here) he breaks the bars of his cage and rips his shirt. This toy was made after the success of the Incredible Hulk TV series. S. Kimball Collection.

brightly-colored **Spider-Man**. (Personally, I think the wall-crawling scenes were great!) The show was doomed to only three or four TV specials and died.

This attempt at live-action Super Heroes programming brought later specials with characters such as **Captain America**, **Doctor Strange**, and **Doc Savage**, as well as **Wonder Woman**. The first **Wonder Woman** was untraditional but the second was a hit to rival even the **Hulk**'s success.

Of course, the Super Hero star of the 1970s was **Superman**. His first movie was a huge success. Unfortunately, later movies relied too heavily on special effects and less on plot development. **Superman** was truly the father of all Super Heroes. His movies of the 1970s and 1980s inspired *Supergirl*, and probably had a helping hand in making *Robocop* believable. The 1980s had its fair share of Super Heroes. **Captain Avenger** was a hero for actor John Ritter in the comedy *Hero at Large*. He was a great true-to-life hero, with no powers but lots of wit. "Sable" tried to make it, as well as "Once a Hero," but Super Heroes became harder to believe in these days of "Miami Vice" and "Cosby."

As has been discussed by collectors and Super Hero fans for years, you just cannot get the public to believe in a strong man in fancy pajamas, which is what this discussion boils down to. **Terminator**, **Robocop**, and even **Tarzan** succeeded in the movies because they fit into their surroundings, even if their environment was not totally realistic. I believe that the key to **Superman's** success was the longevity of the character himself. Just think, his following includes everyone born from 1933 on!

But even **Superman** was swept up in the general tide of Super Heroes in the 1970s. The public did not cry out for a certain hero, it cried out for every hero! That is what Mego Toys gave them: Eight-inch plastic Super Heroes that were bendable, colorful, and easily mangled. Their fragility guaranteed a huge turnover in these figures, making them the hit of the toy industry then and a hit with collectors now.

Mego Toys 8" figures of Marvel Comics' Fantastic Four. Notice the flames on the flying Human Torch, the visibility of the Invisible Girl, the outfit of the rocky Thing, and the proportionate Mr. Fantastic. These are just a few of the Mego "Official World's Greatest Super-Heroes" action figure series. S. Kimball Collection.

MEGO
WORLD'S GREATEST SUPER HEROES

Post-Action Jackson

With the assistance of Mark Huckabone

As the 1970s dawned, Mego toys put their full marketing thrust into the action figure marketplace, which was slowly being vacated by Hasbro's **G. I. Joe.** One of Hasbro's last efforts to revive the line was the **G. I. Joe Action Team** with more accessories than ever before, as well as comic books and a huge television promotion.

After condensing the figure from 12 to 8 inches, Mego launched **Action Jackson** which, in com-

parison to **G. I. Joe,** included twice as many accessories and outfits at half the price.

Action Jackson sold for as little as $2.50 with clothes and accessories priced as low as $1.50! Every kid in America could afford that, no matter how small his allowance.

This **Action Jackson**, by the way, bore no resemblance to the 1988 movie version. **Action**

Hasbro's G. I. Joe (left) as compared with Mego's Action Jackson (right). S. Kimball Collection and photograph.

Jackson outfits were ordinary, not like **G. I. Joe's** military-type costumes. **Action Jackson's** accessory packs included surfboards with matching California jams, as well as clothing for construction workers, scuba divers, and safari members. Little did Mego know that this simple male body form would be used in countless variations with only a color or head change in order to make a different character.

When **Action Jackson** faded in 1974, Mego got another idea — **SUPER HEROES!**

The first series included some of the most popular heroes and villains. **Batman** and **Robin**, **Captain America**, **Superman**, **Aquaman**, **Penguin**, **Mr. Mxyzptlk**, **Joker**, and the **Riddler**.

The figures were mass produced with very few different plastic-injected molds made. The molds for the arms and legs were the same, with all in a flesh tone. The bodies came in two forms; one served as a regular shape for all of the figures, except **Penguin** and **Mr. Mxyzptlk**, who had a pot-bellied mold of their own.

A comparison of the Human Torch with his accompanying blister pack and Action Jackson with his box. S. Kimball Collection.

The figures, like **Action Jackson**, were put together without a great deal of care. The bodies were hollow, with only a thin string of elastic material holding the arms, which were attached through the hollow chest, to the legs, which were attached through the hollow torso. The head was easily pulled off with only a slight twist. The joints at the knee and elbow were thin plastic rivets that put stress on the calves and forearms. Some boxed figures were found on store shelves, already broken, especially at the knee, from handling of the cartons!

The costumes on these figures were very accurate and made of the same polyester cloth that the earlier **Captain Action** figures used. The costumes were decorated with paper-sticker emblems and features, such as capes, were made of a thin woven plastic. The figures of **Batman**, **Robin**, and **Aquaman** came with gloves, and all of the figures came with thin, plastic boots or shoes. **Batman** and **Robin** had removable masks, and other figures may have also had them. With a little imagination and some left-over **Action Jackson** accessories, you could have **Bruce Wayne** and **Dick Grayson**!! (For those not in the know, Bruce and Dick are the Caped Crusaders' alter-egos!)

During the production of these figures there was only one mold change. **Mr. Mxyzptlk** was produced

Close-ups of the Caped Crusaders. Notice the loose-fitting gloves (mittens really) and the removable mask of Batman. J. McGonagle Collection.

Both Superman and Green Arrow show the wide range of appeal of these 8" figures. Superman, from the first series was the "popular" figure. Green Arrow, from the second series, is regarded these days as the best-looking figure of either series by most collectors. J. Mc-Gonagle Collection.

with two different faces. According to Mark Huckabone, the version with **Mr. Mxyzptlk's** mouth closed is the rarer of the two.

The first series was packaged in a box with the character's name in lettering from the comic book, a plastic picture window revealing the figure, and below a red box with white-lettered "WORLD'S GREATEST SUPER-HEROES!" A black outline around the box had "OFFICIAL" tilted at the center. Also printed on the first series boxes was "RECOMMENDED FOR CHILDREN OVER 3 YEARS OLD," as well as a quick description of the character. For instance, **Mr. Mxyzptlk's** reads "SUPERMAN'S Arch Enemy." On the back of the box were cut-out trading cards which accounts for the lack of boxes for collectors these days. On the sides were pictures of all of the characters produced, in a mix of DC and Marvel.

MEGO SUPER HEROES II

Making a Good Thing Better

The mid-1970s were Mego's glory years. The Super Heroes sold very well — well enough to warrant new characters. On the scene came **Shazam (Captain Marvel)**, **Spider-Man**, **Hulk**, **Iron Man**, **Thor**, the **Fantastic Four** — **Human Torch**, **Mr. Fantastic**, **Thing** and the **Invisible Girl**; **Batgirl**, **Wonder Woman**, and **Supergirl**; also the villains, **Lizard** and the **Green Goblin**. (Among this collection of heroes and villains, Mego also produced ac-

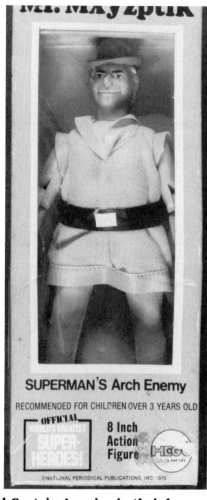

Mr. Mxyzptlk and Captain America in their boxes. Notice the design change in the bottom of the box of the first series (left) from the second series (right). The white star sticker on Captain America's chest has fallen off; most of the stickers used by Mego on their figures deteriorate very rapidly. Photos courtesy of Hake's Americana & Collectibles.

tion figures of **Conan** and **Tarzan**. Though they are not considered Super Heroes, these caracters have been listed in this chapter. For more information about why these two characters, as well as other non-Super Heroes, are generally not discussed in this volume, see the "Less than Action Figures" section.)

Some of these added heroes required new molds. One was made for females, and the **Thing**, the **Lizard**, and the **Hulk** each had an individual body mold. It is rumored that there was a **Rhino** figure that used the **Hulk's** mold, but none have been reported. Another hero, **Green Lantern**, was presumed manufactured, but Mark Huckabone states that it never left the drawing board.

Unlike their predecessors, these figures had thick bands of rubber to hold the arms and legs together, inside the body; however, the knees and elbows still broke easily.

It seemed that as soon as the Mego Super Heroes hit the shelves, they were sold. New characters in-

cluded **Green Arrow, Catwoman, Isis, Falcon, Teen Titans: Aqualad, Kid Flash, Speedy,** and **Wonder Girl**. It is interesting to note that the **Teen Titans** were only seven inches tall as were **Penguin, Mr. Mxyzptlk,** and **Robin**.

When these heroes began to lose popularity in 1975, Mego issued a new set of **Batman, Robin, Joker,** and the **Riddler**, each with "Fist Fighting" action. These four had levers protruding from the back of their costumes which, when activated, made their arms wave.

Mego adapted a different packaging technique, the blister pack, in 1976, which consisted of a thin, plastic bubble (with figure enclosed) glued to a lithographed cardboard sheet. Thus, the figure was even less protected and had a more likely chance of being damaged. It seems some of the figures, such as **Teen Titans**, never saw the insides of a box. Another packaging plan was to package the heroes in different languages for use outside of the United

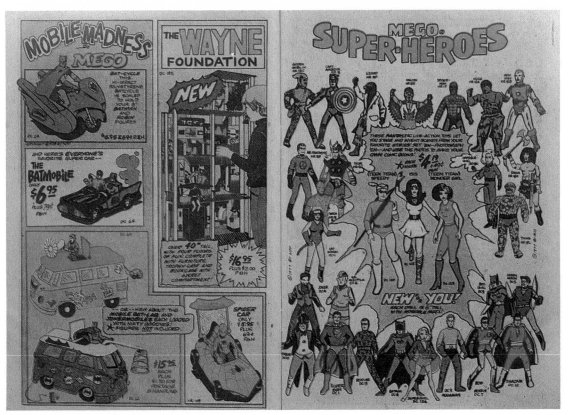

These comic book pages show both accessories and figures from the second series of the Mego 8" action figures.

SHAZAM! (Captain Marvel) and Tarzan give you an idea of the range of characters that Mego thought of as Super Heroes. SHAZAM! (Captain Marvel) is one of the first recognized Super Heroes while Tarzan is rarely thought of as a Super Hero. J. McGonagle Collection.

States. They have only been reported in French and Spanish. Figures found in boxes are now worth much more than those in blister packs. Also, those labeled in English are worth more than the imported boxes in French or Spanish.

If the Super Hero craze wasn't enough, Mego modeled 8" action figures after other characters as well. From the **Dukes of Hazard** and **CHiPS** figures to characters from the **Wizard Of Oz** and **Planet of the Apes**, Mego characterized almost every movie and television star.

To collectors of dolls, these plastic figures are priceless, as well as "a dime-a-dozen." Mego went to great efforts to authenticate the outfits worn by their basic molded figures. The outfits for the **Wizard of Oz** figures, especially, virtually make the movie come to life. The facial expressions on the figures are noted as some of the best ever seen.

Mego also manufactured 12" figures of the rock group, **Kiss**, who, during the 1970s, were infamous for their colorful, fantasy make-up and loud music. **Flash Gordon** and **Ming the Merciless**, along with a variety of other characters associated with **Flash's** comic strip, were also made. These 12" figures will be discussed later in this chapter.

It is fascinating to note the great number of action figure enthusiasts who collect nothing but Mego

Catwoman and Wonder Woman are detailed examples of female Super Hero action figures. Note Catwoman's tail and the ring of cellophane wrapped around her head. The cellophane ring was Mego's way of keeping the figure's hair from becoming tangled. J. McGonagle Collection.

dolls. And it is easy to see why. Many times, a licensing manufacturer pays little attention to design accuracy when duplicating a comic book character. (See some of the **Captain Action** outfits in his chapter for examples of this.) While recent years have seen some improvement in design, Mego was exemplary in closing the gap between the comic book prototype and its replica.

Yet, even Mego has made a few mistakes. This is most notable in the **Fantastic Four** collection. The **Thing** figure, for example, has an orange, rock-printed outfit stretched on his torso, instead of having a bare, molded rock-body. Since all of Mego's male heroes' appear to have been produced from the same torso mold, it was undoubtedly less expensive for the company to produce a **Thing** costume, then a special mold for him.

The rest of the **Fantastic Four** seemed to have produced design problems for Mego, also. **Mr. Fantastic**, who stretches in every direction in the comics, is simply a doll in a blue outfit. An obvious problem with the **Invisible Girl** is that she is fully visible. The **Human Torch** is illustrated in the comics as a figure in flames. The action figure does not have many features, but a series of yellow and red flames.

HEROES LISTING

AQUAMAN: Blonde hair and eyebrows; flesh-toned basic male mold with orange torso, black trunks with large yellow "A" decal and green leotards with green fins on back of calf, thin green mittens. Observed in box. **15   40**

BATGIRL: Long black hair on female face with blue Type 5 mask; flesh-toned basic female mold with gray outfit and gold bat symbol, blue boots; no reported accessories. **15   40**

BATMAN: Blue removable Type 3 mask with points over ears; flesh-toned basic male mold with gray outfit decorated with batsymbol, blue cape, trunks, and boots; thin blue mittens. Observed in box. **30   60**

BATMAN: Mask identical to previous but not removable; outfit identical except without mittens. Observed in box. **15   40**

CAPTAIN AMERICA: Blue Type 3 mask with white A on front; flesh-toned basic male mold with red hands, red, white, and blue outfit, red boots; accessories included red, white, and blue shield. Observed in box. **15   40**

FALCON: Short black hair on black face with red and white Type 5 mask; black flesh-toned basic male mold with white and red outfit, red boots; no reported accessories. **15   40**

GREEN ARROW: Short blonde hair on male face with green Type 1 mask; flesh-toned basic male mold with green and black outfit, black boots; accessories included quiver with arrows and bow. **15   40**

HULK: Black hair on grimacing green face; green flesh-toned extra-muscled mold with torn magenta pants and rope belt; no reported accessories. Observed in blister packs. **12   25**

IRON MAN: Crimson and gold helmet; red basic male mold with crimson and gold outfit detailed like metal, red boots. **15   40**

ISIS: Long black hair on female face with tiara; flesh-toned basic female mold with white gown and golden belt, black boots. **20   50**

ROBIN: Black removable Type 1 mask, black hair; flesh-toned basic male mold with red outfit and black **Robin** symbol, yellow Type 4 cape with Type 1 collar, green trunks and boots; thin green mittens. Observed in box. **30   60**

ROBIN: Mask identical to previous but not removable; outfit identical but without mittens. Observed in box. **15   40**

SHAZAM (Captain Marvel): Short black hair and eyebrows; flesh-toned basic male mold with red and yellow body suit, yellow cape and boots; no accessories reported. Observed in box.   **12   25**

SPIDER-MAN: Red Type 4 mask with white and black eyelets; red basic male mold with red, black, and blue body suit. Observed in blister pack.   **12   25**

SUPERGIRL: Long blonde hair on female face; flesh-toned basic female mold with red and blue outfit, red boots and cape.   **20   50**

SUPERMAN: Black hair with cowlick and eyebrows; flesh-toned basic male mold with red and blue body suit, red cape and boots. Observed in box.   **15   40**

THOR: Long blonde hair and eyebrows with gray cap; flesh-toned basic male mold with blue outfit, yellow boots and red cape; accessories included gray and brown square hammer.   **20   50**

WONDER WOMAN: Long black hair on female face; flesh-toned basic female mold with red and yellow bodice, blue shorts with field of white stars, red boots; accessories included golden lasso.   **20   50**

THE FANTASTIC FOUR: Each were sold separately, never as a set.

Human Torch — Red head with yellow embossed flames; red basic male mold with red outfit with black and yellow detailed flames; no accessories reported. Observed in blister pack.   **12   25**

Invisible Girl — Long blonde hair on female face; flesh-toned basic female mold with blue, black, and white body suit, black boots; no accessories reported. Observed in blister pack.   **20   50**

Mr. Fantastic — Short black hair with white at temples; flesh-toned basic male mold with blue, black, and white body suit, black boots; no accessories reported. Observed in blister pack.   **15   40**

Thing — Orange rocky face with blue eyes and open mouth; orange extra-muscled body with rocky fists and rocky-detailed cloth outfit with blue trunks; no accessories reported. Observed in blister pack.   **15   40**

TEEN TITANS: Quite rare figures; all 7" tall. Each were sold separately, never as a set.

Aqualad — Black hair and eyebrows, flesh-toned basic male mold with red tunic and green briefs and shoes; no accessories reported.   **20   50**

Kid Flash — Yellow Type 3 cowl on head with red wings on sides of head; flesh-toned basic male mold with yellow body suit and red boots; no accessories reported.   **20   50**

Speedy — Black hair and eyebrows with Type 1 green mask; flesh-toned basic male mold with red tunic, green pants, and black boots; accessories included quiver of arrows and bow.   **20   50**

Wonder Girl — Black long hair and eyebrows, flesh-toned basic female mold with red body suit decorated with field of yellow stars, red boots; accessories included golden lasso.   **20   50**

VILLAINS LISTING

CATWOMAN: Long black hair on female head; flesh-toned basic female mold with gray outfit and black boots; no accessories reported.   **15   40**

GREEN GOBLIN: Green face with magenta stocking-cap; green basic male mold with magenta outfit and boots; accessories included black flying bat.   **12   25**

JOKER: White face with green hair and red lips; white basic male mold with white and purple body suit and purple jacket with tales. Observed in box.   **15   40**

LIZARD: Green reptilian face; green basic male mold with reptillian tale at rear; white lab coat over black turtleneck; no accessories reported.   **12   25**

MR. MXYZPTLK: Magenta top hat on face with large nose; flesh-toned obese body mold with orange bodice and large black belt. Observed in box.   **15   40**

The Joker figure without his box or shoes. Notice the printing detail of a shirt, vest, and pants on one body suit. Photograph courtesy of Hake's Americana & Collectibles.

The Penguin is shown in profile. Notice the extended nose and pot belly. S. Kimball Collection.

PENGUIN: Black top hat on face with large nose; flesh-toned obese body mold with white hands, purple and white body suit with black jacket and tales. Observed in box and blister pack.   12   25

RIDDLER: Black hair and magenta Type 1 mask; flesh-toned male mold with green hands, green body suit with purple belt and black question marks all over. Observed in box.   15   40

NOT SO SUPER, HEROES LISTING

CONAN: Long black hair on head; flesh-toned basic male mold with tattered brown outfit; accessories included knife and large axe.   12   25

TARZAN: Black hair and eyebrows; flesh-toned basic male mold with leapord skin costume; accessories included knife and belt.   12   25

SUPER HEROES' ALTER EGOS

These figures were mail-in offers, sold by J. C. Penney during the 1974 Christmas season. Both sets were mailed in plain brown boxes.

SET 1: (price is for set with box)   270   300
Bruce Wayne — Flesh-toned basic male mold with short black hair; dressed in black dinner jacket and white slacks.   85   125
Dick Grayson — Flesh-toned basic male mold with short black hair; dressed in red pullover sweater and blue jeans.   85   125

SET 2: (price is for set with box)   270   300
Clark Kent — Flesh-toned basic male mold with short black hair (without front curl); dressed in blue two-piece suit and eyeglasses.   85   125
Peter Parker — Flesh-toned basic male mold with short brown hair; dressed in outfit similar to **Dick Grayson's**, exact details unknown.   85   125

FIGHTING FIST HEROES LISTING

BATMAN: Identical to earlier Mego **Batman**, but with Fighting Fist action.   NRS

ROBIN: Identical to earlier Mego **Robin**, but with Fighting Fist action.   NRS

JOKER: Identical to earlier Mego **Joker**, but with Fighting Fist action.   NRS

RIDDLER: Identical to earlier Mego **Riddler**, but with Fighting Fist action.   NRS

ACCESSORIES

AQUAMAN VS. THE GREAT WHITE SHARK: 8" **Aquaman** figure and white shark with opening jaws and red propeller at the tail. When activated, the shark's jaws opened when it ran into another object. Cardboard insert had undersea illustration in which the shark was placed; **Aquaman** was mounted above in a swimming position among cardboard waves and was held with plastic twisters.   NRS

BATCAVE: 15" x 15" x 11-1/4" cardboard and vinyl playset. Included Batcave secret entrance which resembled 1960's TV show version; red Bat computer; single Batpole; roof-mounted flashing Batsignal spotlight.   80   120

The Batcave is an extraordinary Mego accessory with many features. J. McGonagle Collection.

BATCYCLE: Black cycle with sets and gray handlebars and engine. Came with detachable black sidecar with three vertical gray jets. The sidecar was not like that of the TV Series... it was not a "Go-Cart." "**BATMAN**" within Batsymbol decal was applied to back fin of cycle and on side of sidecar. A profile of **Batman** was centered on the wind guard.   **35   50**

BATCOPTER: Black and red Batcopter resembled a two-colored shoe. Four small wheels underneath; red propeller; black stabalizer. "**BATMAN**" within Batsymbol decal was applied to hood.   **35   50**

BATMOBILE: Black Batmobile was duplicate of Batmobile used in the 1960's TV show. The body was shortened and fit two figures. "**BATMAN**" within Batsymbol decal was applied to both doors.   **45   70**

The Batcycle is one of the few accessories for the 8" Mego figures. Photo courtesy of Hake's Americana and Collectibles.

Penguin, Wonder Woman, and the Joker make up some of the Mego Pocket Super Heroes. Notice the change in packaging between the villains and the heroine. J. McGonagle Collection.

CAPTAIN AMERICAR: Blue car with flipping traditional Captain America shield. **"CAPTAIN AMERICA"** lettered on each side of car.   **40**   **65**

GREEN ARROWCAR: Green car with two yellow ball-tip darts flanking the driver's seat and one loaded into the arrow launcher under the hood.   **45**   **70**

HALL OF JUSTICE PLAYSET: Translocation chamber inside moved action figure from the entrance to a screen with a see-through middle, making it appear as if the figure was at a different scene; dial console showed up to six villains, cities, and times of disaster; conference table had maps on top and removable cardboard sides. Also came with Hall of Justice sign for top of playset, instruction sheet, and Mego mini-catalogue.   **NRS**

JOKERMOBILE: Green Volkswagen bus with various decals. Squeeze-bulb squirter flower on roof, rear-end boxing glove trap, and revolving observation deck inside.   **50**   **80**

MOBILE BAT-LAB: Black Volkswagen bus with various decals. Yellow cage Battrap on roof, rear-end Bat-wench with grappling hook, and revolving observation deck inside.   **50**   **80**

SPIDER-CAR: Red car with black web trim and spider on hood; spoiler with the traditional decal lettered "The AMAZING **SPIDER-MAN**". Webbing attached from bottom of spoiler to back of car.   **45**   **70**

SUPER ACTION FLYBY SUPERVATOR: Included red and green clamp; green Supervator with yellow secret hanger and Super Hero alarm; red and white flyby harness with secret backpack; three double-sided villain cards (e.g., **Riddler/Mr. Mxyzptlk**, **Joker/Penguin**, **Green Goblin/Jungle Chief**); Z-magic blue gloves with velcro; red handle with plastic string; instruction sheet; and Mego catalogue. According to collector Mark Huckabone, **Jungle Chief** was a Mego-created villain.   **NRS**

WAYNE FOUNDATION: Over 40" tall with four floors. Made of vinyl and cardboard with plastic supports. Included furniture, trophy case and bookcase with secret compartment.   **80**   **120**

MEGO 3-3/4" SUPER HEROES

Heroes for your pocket

To some, the word Mego means only 8" figures. However, there are 3-3/4" Mego action figures with very complex accessories. After shrinking the 8" dolls and changing the materials used, new figures, called Comic Action Heroes, came to life. The three sets offered were:

This box contains Batman, Robin, and a Batmobile that resembles the Batmobile of the 1960s. J. McGonagle Collection.

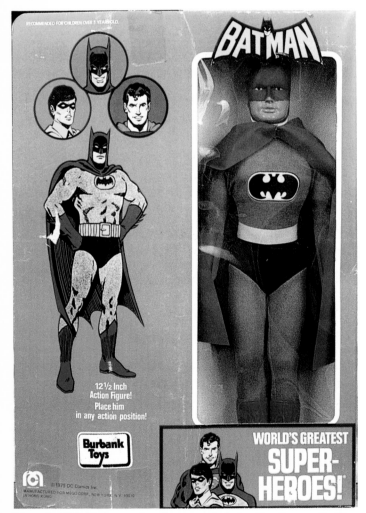

Mego's 12" Batman is shown mint in the box. J. McGonagle Collection.

• **Wonder Woman** and the exploding tower, with invisible jet;

• **Batman** and **Robin** and the exploding bridge, with Batmobile;

• **Superman** and the exploding Fortress of Solitude.

The figures of **Wonder Woman**, **Batman**, and **Robin** are all in a frozen with bent knees into a semi-squatting position; therefore, they are not action figures, and came with a plastic stand. In the second series of production, new figures were added to the sets. For example, **Joker** and the **Penguin** were added to the **Batman** and **Robin** exploding bridge set.

*"The **Caped Crusaders** ride the Batmobile over what will be an exploding bridge... if the **Joker** and the **Penguin** have anything to do with it!"*

The effect of exploding was produced by dropping the lever of a plastic plunger which forced air through a tube into a deflated accordion-type of pump. When the pump was inflated, it upset whatever was on top of it.

After a year of production, Mego returned to what previously made so many sales on the market — a large selection of true action figures.

The Pocket Super Heroes came out without fanfare. The figures were true action figures that moved at the head, shoulders, and waist, without a stand. The first packaging was in a dark red package with color script lettering. The first heroes included **Batman**, **Superman**, **Robin**, **Wonder Woman**, **Spider-Man**, **Captain America**, **Shazam (Captain Marvel)**, **Penguin**, **Joker**, **Lex Luthor**, and the **Green Goblin**.

New packaging was on a larger, white board with more illustrations and the blister pack with hero/villain moved to the right bottom instead of centered at the bottom. Also, in the new packages were added **Aquaman**, **Green Lantern**, **General Zod**, and **Jor-El**.

The Spider-Machine travels over any terrain. S. Kimball Collection.

Lex Luthor and Superman, part of Mego's 12" action figure series, are shown in their mint boxes. J. McGonagle Collection.

Jor-El and **General Zod**, were two characters from the first two **Superman** movies which were released just before these figures were manufactured. **Jor-El** is **Superman's** Kryptonian father, and **General Zod** is a renegade would-be ruler of Krypton, who Councilman **Jor-El** sent to the phantom zone just prior to Krypton's destruction.

There were many new accessories in the second run. More Batmobiles and invisible jets were manufactured, which were of the same molds as the original Comic Action Heroes. There were many other vehicles and buildings including the Batcave, The Hall of Justice, the Mangler, Batmachine, Spider Machine, and Spider Car. Many of the accessories, such as the Spider Car, came with heroes — the Spider Car came with **Spider-Man** and the **Hulk**.

3-3/4" MEGO ACTION HEROES LISTING

WONDER WOMAN: Included unbendable figure of **Wonder Woman**, transparent plastic jet, collapsible tower, and plunger activator. **25   50**

BATMAN: Included unbendable figures of **Batman** and **Robin**, black 1960s-style Batmobile, collapsible bridge, and plunger activator. **25   50**

BATMAN: Identical to previous listing but included unbendable figures of **Penguin** and **Joker**. **35   60**

SUPERMAN: Included unbendable figure of **Superman**, Fortress of Solitude playset with falling walls, and plunger activator. **25   50**

POCKET SUPER HEROES LISTING

BATMAN: Traditional outfit.	**7**	**15**
SUPERMAN: Traditional outfit.	**7**	**15**
ROBIN: Traditional outfit.	**7**	**15**
WONDER WOMAN: Traditional outfit.	**7**	**15**
SPIDER-MAN: Traditional outfit.	**7**	**15**
CAPTAIN AMERICA: Traditional outfit.	**7**	**15**
SHAZAM (CAPTAIN MARVEL): Traditional outfit.	**7**	**15**
HULK: Traditional outfit.	**10**	**25**
AQUAMAN: Traditional outfit.	**10**	**25**
GREEN LANTERN: Traditional outfit.	**10**	**25**
JOR-EL: Traditional outfit.	**7**	**15**
PENGUIN: Traditional outfit.	**7**	**15**

JOKER: Traditional outfit.   7   15

LEX LUTHOR: Traditional outfit.   7   15

GREEN GOBLIN: Traditional outfit.   7   15

GENERAL ZOD: 7   15

POCKET SUPER HEROES ACCESSORIES LISTING

BATMOBILE: 1960s style.   NRS

INVISIBLE JET: Transparent plastic.   NRS

BATCAVE: Details unknown.   NRS

HALL OF JUSTICE: Computer detail on walls, translocation chamber, map table, crime computer.   NRS

THE MANGLER: Bulldozer with large alligator-type snout with square teeth. Tongue inside of mouth. Came with villain card.   NRS

BATMACHINE: Details unknown.   NRS

SPIDER-MACHINE: Large red tractor-type vehicle with computer programmable memory system on board. Many colorful decals included.   **15   35**

SPIDER CAR: Details unknown, came with **Spider-Man** and **Hulk** features.   **NRS**

MEGO 12" SUPER HEROES

"Enough, already!"

The 8" **Action Jackson** and succeeding Super Heroes seem to take off where the 12" **G. I. JOE** left off; however, the demise of the 12" action figure was short-lived. In the late 1970s, Mego manufactured a small amount of 12" action figures. They included characters from the **Superman** movies, the **Flash Gordon** comics, and the **Buck Rogers** television show. There were also the Super Heroes **Wonder Woman**, **Batman**, **Robin**, and **Spider-Man**.

Little information has been received regarding this 12" series. Reader input would be appreciated.

The Remco Energized Batman and Batman Climbing Figure make up two miscellaneous 1970s figures. J. McGonagle Collection.

MISCELLANEOUS 1970s FIGURES

Some of the "off-the-wall" singular figures are listed at the end of each chapter. The following figures may not represent action figures but are of interest to Super Hero action figure collectors. We would like to thank *Hake's Americana & Collectibles* for assisting with descriptions and photographs of some of the following items.

There are many toy action figures that were made in small numbers. We hope to find them all and list them in future editions of this book. Please fill in the correction/addition form attached to the inside front cover to help us in this ongoing research.

LISTINGS

STATUES: 1977; Marx, 6" tall, 100 percent plastic. Originally $4.39 for the set as advertised in an August Marvel Comic.

(A) **Daredevil**.	15	30
(B) **Hulk**.	15	30
(C) **Captain America**.	15	30
(D) **Iron Man**.	15	30
(E) **Spider-Man**.	15	30
(F) **Thor**.	15	30

PARACHUTIST TOY (AHI): 1974; 4" tall molded plastic figure with attached thin plastic parachute; figure was weighted so that it would float to the ground in parachute fashion after being tossed into the air. This toy was one in a series. Reader information is requested. Courtesy Hake's Americana & Collectibles.

(A) **Penguin**.	10	25
(B) **Batman**.	10	25
(C) **Robin**.	10	25
(D) **Joker**.	10	25

MEGO SUPER HEROES BENDIES: 1972-74; 5" tall plastic figures with wire skeletons to bend (like Mattel's **Matt Mason**). Reader information is requested.

(A)	**Batman**.	10	20
(B)	**Robin**.	10	20
(C)	**Superman**.	10	20
(D)	**Aquaman**.	10	20
(E)	**Shazam**. (Captain Marvel)	10	20
(F)	**Tarzan**.	10	20
(G)	**Spider-Man**.	10	20
(H)	**Captain America**.	10	20
(I)	**Batgirl**.	10	20
(J)	**Supergirl**.	10	20
(K)	**Wonder Woman**.	10	20
(L)	**Catwoman**.	10	20
(M)	**Joker**.	10	20
(N)	**Riddler**.	10	20

(O)	**Penguin**.	10	20
(P)	**Mr. Mxyzptlk**.	10	20

REMCO ENERGIZED SUPER HEROES: 1978; 12" battery-operated hard-shell dolls. More reader information requested.

(A)	**Superman**.	NRS
(B)	**Batman**.	NRS
(C)	**Spider-Man**.	NRS
(D)	**Green Goblin**.	NRS

A smaller 9" tall set of **Batman**, **Superman**, and **Captain America** figures by Remco came out at the same time as the 12" ones. More reader information requested.

NRS

These figures are just a few of the many designed by the author for his collection. From left to right are The Human Torch, Silver Surfer, D-Man, Hawkeye, Captain Marv-ell, The Captain, Vision, Vanguard, Captain Britain, Machine Man, Cyclops, Nightcrawler, Taskmaster, Nomad, Colossus, and The Punisher. S. Kimball Collection.

THE 1980s

From Mutants to Dark Knights

It seems that the 1980s will be noted in toy and comic book history as the decade in which the toys dictated comic characters. When **Spider-Man**, **Batman**, **Captain America**, and **Superman** were marketed, no one was surprised; these four characters probably hold the largest number of licenses in the Super Hero world. Everyone collecting comics wanted to collect this memorabilia. But, then look what happened...

When a deal was struck between the licensee and the copyright holder, the relationship between comic and toy was turned upside down. Take a long look at **Batman**. When the TV series became highly rated prime time entertainment, the comics created a new, "campy" **Batman**. Soon there were pratfalls, strange colors, and the appearance of new criminal personalities in the comics. After the show was canceled, **Batman** again became a detective and has recently been dubbed "The Dark Knight."

In the 1980s some comics reflected the licensing preferences of the toy industry. Of course a few of the toy-related comic series were good, in spite of the annoying appearance of the newly-created toy vehicles. **Secret Wars I** was a landmark series for Marvel Comics because almost all of their characters put in an appearance. But **Secret Wars II** and its "millions" of crossover comics became more tedious than entertaining. DC Comics achieved the same dubious result in each of its three crossover series, **Super Powers**, **Crisis on Infinite Earths**, and the most recent, **Millennium** series.

Most of these comics which originated from toys lost value in story, art, or characterizations. **Captain Action** was the first to suffer this fate in the late 1960s, with only five comic issues to its credit. **Defenders of the Earth**, on the other hand, was a great TV Show, but not a great comic. Apparently some of these figures should have been left alone; but, then again, comics are where most Super Heroes got their start. (See the toy-turned-comic discussion that follows the miscellaneous listing at the end of this 1980s preview.) Unless, of course, you happened to mention folks like **Thundercats**, **Tigersharks**, **Astroboy**, **Underdog**, **Mighty Heroes**, **Silverhawks**, **Transformers**, **G. I. Joe**, etc... (I could go on forever).

At the time of this writing, a few of these TV show-turned-comic books have started looking good! The **Underdog**, **Thundercats**, and **Space Ghost** comics are particularly outstanding. While only the

Thundercats have fostered their own line of toys, some comic book collectors have grown tired of the trend towards the promotion of a new TV show, followed by commercials for the tie-in toys, and then immediately seeing the "Comic Adaptation" of the series!

However, with the recent expansion of Super Hero figures in the toy industry, less traditional characters are also finding their way into the stores. With Marvel's **X-Men** being one of the top-rated comics of all time, surely figures based on this series would sell like crazy. And, apparently, Marvel has recognized

this and will launch an **X-Men** action figure series in late 1988.

MICELLANEOUS 1980s ACTION FIGURES

NEW ACTIVATED SUPER HEROES COLLECTION SET: 1983; originally $7.50 for each of two sets as advertised in a June Marvel Comic. Each set had five plastic figures, with action hands that gripped and slid down a string via Super Heroes activator.

(A) **Set 888111 — Falcon, Human Torch, Doctor Doom, Spider-Man, and Green Goblin.**   15   30

These two photographs show a set of Marvel Comics' figures produced in Spain. All of these figures have the Marvel Comics copyright symbol. Notice the eyes on She-Hulk and the stance of Captain America. S. Maged Collection.

(B) **Set 888112** — **Submariner**, **Captain America**, **Thor**, **Dr. Octopus**, and **Red Skull**.   15   30

SPANISH MARVEL FIGURES: 1987; previously unknown figures made in Spain; made of heavy rubber, authentic painting schemes, except for **Spider-Woman** (see photos); average 3" tall. Set price: 100   150

(A) **Captain America** — Traditional red, white, and blue costume with to-scale shield. Figure held shield close to torso, one arm raised in a fist; face had silly smile.
                                                                                         10   20

(B) **Doctor Doom** — Traditional robe, belt, and holster. Figure held up silver goblet.   10   20

(C) **Hulk** — Traditional green skin with torn magenta pants. Figure had over-sized hands; one hand was raised as if to hold something up.
                                                                                         10   20

(D) **Iron Man** — Traditional crimson and gold colors. Walking figure.   10   20

(E) **She-Hulk** — Traditional green skin with torn white jump suit. Figure position was similar to **Spider-Woman** figure; face had big pixie-type eyes with Oriental slant.
                                                                                         10   20

(F) **Spider-Man** — Traditional Type 1 outfit but web details were etched into figure instead of black-printed

MARVEL LICENSING

An advertisement from Marvel Comics in the trade magazine Toy & Hobby. Note the announcement of the new X-Men series.

webbing. Figure was in crouched position, both arms outspread.   10   20

(G) **Spider-Woman** — Blue with red trim, very untraditional colors. Black webbing under arms on transparent wing. Figure had one arm raised as if to wave.
                                                                                         10   20

(H) **Thor** — Traditonal colors. Figure had raised arms, held mystic hammer, Moljinar, in right hand.   10   20

Collector John McGonagle created these characters from various 12" figures. From left to right are Michael (from the movie *Halloween*), Captain Scarlett, Joker, Green Arrow, Dick Tracy, and Sable. J. McGonagle Collection.

On the planet of the Beyonder, where the Marvel Secret Wars take place, we see (left to right) the evil Kang, Doctor Doom, and the Constrictor versus our heroes Captain America, Spider-Man, and Wolverine. The Marvel Super Heroes Secret Wars collection is manufactured by Mattel Toys, Inc. S. Kimball Collection.

MARVEL SUPER HEROES SECRET WARS

Super Heroes following a script

"**C**an the combined might of Earth's most *powerful Super Heroes defeat the ultimate menace?!!*" blurbed the comic book, **Marvel Super Heroes Secret Wars** issue No. 1.

According to the Marvel Hype Box in May 1984's comics, *"The debut of this twelve-issue limited series was not only the biggest event of the month, but it's the most important series Marvel will publish this year!!"*

And right they were! This was the second series Marvel had undertaken which featured most of the characters in the Marvel Universe. The first series of this type was produced in 1982 and was called the **Contest of Champions**. It seems that the plots in these series, as well as the many **Super Powers** series and **Crisis** and **Millennium** series that DC Comics produced, followed one of three themes:

- Heroes pitted against each other.
- Heroes pitted against a horde of villains.
- Heroes pitted against a threatening unknown entity.

In the **Secret Wars**, the heroes and villains were pitted against each other on another planet. They were spirited there by the **Beyonder**, a god-like entity. **Secret Wars** characters included the mighty **Avengers: Captain America, Wasp, Thor, She-Hulk, Hawkeye, Iron Man**, and a new **Captain Marvel; X-Men: Storm, Nightcrawler, Rogue, Cyclops, Wolverine, Colossus**, and **Lockeed**, the dragon. Also appearing were three of the **Fantastic Four: Mr. Fantastic**, the **Human Torch**, and the **Thing**. (The **Invisible Girl** was in a "family way" at the time and could not make it.) Also included were the amazing **Spider-Man** and the incredible **Hulk**.

With all of these heroes to choose from, Marvel/Mattel picked the following characters to be manufactured in the first series: **Captain America**, **Iron Man**, **Wolverine**, and **Spider-Man**. During the comic's twelve issues, **Spider-Man's** outfit changed from the traditional blue and red to a black and white version (issue No. 8). The action figure reflected this change in Mattel's second series. It seems *incredible* that a popular hero like the **Hulk** was not selected. Perhaps the size of the **Hulk** in comparison to the other figures explains his exclusion, since it would require a special mold of its own. (Body size did not bother Mego toys when they produced the **Hulk**. He was simply given the same body size as the rest of the male Super Heroes.) Mattel tried to stay "true to the comics" when it came to body size. As discussed later in this chapter, there were only minor anatomical changes on each figure.

The second series of action figures produced were **Captain America** (who remained unchanged), **Spider-Man** (in his temporary new outfit), and the following which were added to the series but never appeared in the **Secret Wars** comics: **Falcon**, **Daredevil**, and **Iceman**.

Each figure was listed in both series according to the order on the backs of blister packs. The villains were treated similarly to the heroes with only a few characters becoming action figures.

In the comics, by a twist of fate, the evil master of magnetism, **Magneto**, ended up on the hero's side. By the end of the first issue, **Magneto** left the group. He was featured as a "fourth party" in the second issue (**Galactus** was the other lone party). **Magneto** later befriended the **Wasp**, then alienated her and befriended his mortal enemies, the **X-Men**. Later, he almost joined forces with **Doctor Doom**, but changed his mind and ended up siding with the heroes for the rest of the series. Nonetheless, the action figure of **Magneto** was listed as a "Marvel Super Villain," complete with a villain's secret shield. The complete comic's roster of **Secret Wars** villains was: **Enchantress**, **Ultron**, **Absorbing Man**, **Wrecker**,

This is the cover for the first issues of both Secret Wars sagas. S. Kimball Collection. Copyright ©**1984/1986/1988 Marvel Entertainment Group, Inc. All Rights Reserved.**

These two panels were from page 25 of issue No. 7 of the Secret Wars II saga. These panels are the only known accounts of the characters Hobgoblin and Electro during the comic book series, although both figures are manufactured by Mattel. S. Kimball Collection. Copyright 1986/1988 Marvel Entertainment Group, Inc. All Rights Reserved.

Thunderball, **Piledriver**, **Bulldozer**, **Kang**, **Galactus**, **the Lizard**, **Molecule Man**, **Doctor Octopus**, and of course, **Doctor Doom**.

Mattel manufactured the following villains: **Doctor Doom**, **Kang**, and **Doctor Octopus**. Once again, the second series included villains that were not seen in the **Secret Wars** comics, namely **Baron Zemo** and **Constrictor**. Besides the unusual choice of heroes and villains, other changes in the comics did not affect the figures (except for **Spider-Man**). From issue Nos. 1 through 9, **Doctor Doom** was depicted in his flowing-robe outfit. Only in issues 10 through 12 did his outfit change. But the action figure was only manufactured in the later, untraditional, costume.

Another lead villain, **Klaw**, later appeared in the comics but never as an action figure. The same thing happened to the new **Spider-Woman** whose black and white costume matched **Spider-Man's** new one. **Iron Man** was also changed in the comic (issue No. 9), but this change was never adapted to the action figure.

SECRET WARS II

The Dawn of the Crossover

In July 1985 the comics again depicted the scenes of heroes versus villains, with the **Beyonder** as a corporate form which caused a ruckus on Earth in his search for "the true meaning of life." There were nine

Daredevil is shown here in pieces to demonstrate how the Secret Wars figures were put together. S. Kimball Collection.

Several different torso designs are used in the molding of Secret Wars Figures. From left to right are Type 1 (Captain America), Type 2 (Wolverine), and Type 3 (Spider-Man). It should be noted that Iron Man has a unique torso design, as does Doctor Doom. S. Kimball Collection.

issues in all, with story lines that crossed over into several different main line comics along the way. All of the heroes from the first **Secret Wars** were involved. A major difference was that **Magneto** had changed outfits and was now leader of the **X-Men** and headmaster of their proteges, the **New Mutants**. At this time, Mattel was still manufacturing **Secret Wars** figures. From **Alpha Flight** to **Power Pack**, just about every character in the **Marvel Universe** was seen in the comics. Alas, no new action figures were manufactured.

A hoard of villains attacked the **Thing** in issue No. 7 and other than that, villains played hardly any role in the series. In this attack on the **Thing**, both **Hobgoblin** and **Electro** appeared. It was their only showing in the entire **Secret Wars** sagas! After following the development of the comic series versus the action figures, two interesting facts are noted: (a) Some of the characters who played major roles in the comics (i.e. **Molecule Man** and the **Human Torch**) were not manufactured, but could have been, and (b) **Daredevil**, **Falcon**, **Iceman**, **Constrictor**, and **Baron Zemo** *never* appeared in either **Secret Wars** saga, but were produced and labeled as **Secret Wars** action figures nonetheless. This raises the baffling question of just why certain figures were made, others changed, and still others overlooked.

THE FIGURES

The 1984 Mattel Toys catalogue featured most of the figures in the **Secret Wars** collection.

"The **Marvel Super Heroes** *were threatened with domination and destruction by Earth's deadliest enemies, the* **Marvel Super Villains**. *It was a time when they must battle for power through the use of secret messages.* **Captain America** *and his allies lead the battle for good against* **Doctor Doom** *and his evil cohorts.*"

The 4-1/4" figures were movable at the neck, shoulders, and hips. Each hero came with a red circular shield and each villain came with a gray square shield. Some characters came with black plastic weapons or accessories unique to the character.

The figures were primarily of the same body shape. There were minor changes in the upper torso, as pictured in the accompanying photograph. The only other changes were in the costume design. You will also notice that the legs and feet on these figures also

Notice the gloves/gauntlets on these figures. At least one hand on these figures is always open, the other is either fisted or open. From left to right are Captain America, Doctor Doom, and Daredevil. S. Kimball Collection.

Shown here are the three European figures (left to right): Iceman, Constrictor, and Electro. Also featured are the illustrated catalogue, blister packs, and Secret Shields for each. S. Kimball Collection.

came in a variety of styles, giving each hero his own particular stance.

During the years the figures were manufactured, they sold for $4 to $6 and in 1986 you could get them for close-out prices from $.99 to $2. At the writing of this book, in late 1988, most figures have become difficult to find, and the accessories almost impossible.

There are three specific figures in the series that are especially rare. The hero **Iceman** and villains **Constrictor** and **Electro** can only be found in Europe. Reported sightings of these three figures in American toy stores are usually attributed to their import from Europe. All have been found with either French or Spanish printing on the blister packs and have the same blister pack backs as the second series figures. Unlike other figures in the second series, the three European figures also had a small, illustrated catalogue inside with a short biography of every character in the series. These biographies included the same information as was on the backs of the various corresponding blister packs.

Included on one side of the fold-out catalogue were **Captain America**, **Falcon**, **Iron Man**, Type 1 **Spider-Man**, **Iceman**, **Wolverine**, and a Type 2 **Spider Man** (who, for some unknown reason, had a different biography than the Type 1 **Spider-Man**). On the last three pages was a coupon for a book that resembled a **Secret Wars** coloring/activity book. On the back

side of the catalogue was an order blank followed by the biographies of **Daredevil**, **Doctor Doom**, **Constrictor**, **Electro**, **Magneto**, **Doctor Octopus**, **Kang**, **Hobgoblin**, and **Baron Zemo**.

From toy collector/dealer Steve Maged, who went to Europe earlier in the year, came word that there were very few, if any, **Icemen**, **Electros**, and **Constrictors** on the shelves of western Europe. He said that in 1986-87 there were plenty of these figures, but now it takes an extensive search to find one.

Certain **Secret Wars** figures, like the **Super Powers** figures in the next chapter, were found in huge quantities, while others were very rare. That explains the inexpensive price for a **Kang** figure which can still be found on toy store shelves, and the high price for an **Iceman** who cannot be found! During the 1984-86 run of these figures, each was usually sold separately in blister packs. The figures were packed in boxes of either 36 heroes or 36 villains (assorted).

Captain America and **Doctor Doom** were sold as one set, Secret Shields included. Collector and dealer Jim Carlo commented that he had heard of three-to-a-pack sets of the figures. Jim saw them only in Sterns Department Stores in New Jersey. Another collector reported the three-packs sold with a picture of **Iceman** on the back, but never saw the actual figure in a three-pack. *READER RESPONSE REQUESTED.* There was also a rumor at the 1987-88 New York International Toy Fair that Marvel will put out more figures of the **X-Men** and possibly an action figure series called **The Marvel Universe**. These figures are reportedly due out in late 1989.

SECRET SHIELDS: The shields were made of a sturdy plastic embossed outline, with a center made of a translucent "flicker" or "videomatic" material that changed the enclosed picture to two different scenes. The shields, *"capable of deciphering secret messages,"* came with eight secret messages on four shield inserts. The gray square shields were 1-3/4" x 1-3/4" with a 1-1/4" x 1-1/4" plastic window. The red circular shield was 1-3/4" in diameter with a 1-1/4" plastic window. The punched-out picture insert was just larger than the window, with a notch

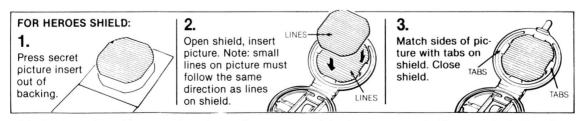

This is the printed instruction sheet that comes with the Secret Shields. S. Kimball Collection.

cut out of the paper that lined up and fit over a plastic peg on the inside of the shield. These notches and pegs not only held the insert firmly against the shield, but lined up the illustration with the grooved lines on the window. This perfect alignment allowed for the flicker-message to change.

By pinching the "key," which opened the shield on a thin hinge, you slipped the secret message inside. When you closed the shield and tilted it, a message appeared and when tilted, changed again. Open the shield and turn the message over. Close and tilt the shield and two different messages appeared.

There were two types of shields: The round, red shield was the heroes' shield and had a round "key" at one end. The circular frame had gear-like embossed and cut-out notches which held the round plastic windows. The square, gray shield was the villain's shield and had a rectangular flat "key" at one end. The square frame had a set of three embossed rivets on all sides with a rounded diamond-shaped hole in each corner. The shield's plastic-edged key opened secret compartments in various vehicles and accessories.

The two types of weapons, rifle (top) and pistol (bottom). S. Kimball Collection.

WEAPONS: Two types of black plastic guns, each with a side piece to clip on to various figures.

The hero shield with various flasher inserts. S. Kimball Collection.

The villain shield with various flasher inserts. S. Kimball Collection.

Doctor Doom with the guns supplied with the figure. S. Kimball Collection.

Type A: Pistol, 1-1/4" x 3/4", a two-barrel that became a pointed barrel with sight. Every villain but **Dr. Octopus** and **Hobgoblin** had one, **Iron Man** oddly enough was the only hero to carry one. In the comics, **Iron Man** rarely needed a weapon, as was also the case with every villain, except **Baron Zemo**.

Type B: Rifle, 2-1/4" x 1-1/4", had one barrel and an extra banana clip underneath as well as a shoulder butt. Only **Doctor Doom** came with one.

VEHICLES AND ACCESSORIES

Each vehicle or accessory came with some sort of secret panel that could be opened with the appropriate key on the accessory or on secret shields.

FREEDOM FIGHTER

The **Freedom Fighter** was the base of operations for the heroes and consisted of a Gunnery Chair, a Radar Chair, and a landing pad for the Turbocopter. This black plastic 25" diameter base of operations was actually a vehicle which rotated when pushed forward. With the highest gunnery chair mounted upright, it was 16" tall.

The **Landing Pad** had the emblem decal of **Captain America**, the red, white, and blue star design on an embossed black dish. It sat on a one-inch tall black plastic mount.

The **Gunnery Chair** was red with a movable double-barreled laser cannon mounted on the front of the chair. The chair itself was on a swivel and mounted on a six-inch black plastic mount.

The **Radar Chair** was blue with a large movable black radar dish mounted on the front. The chair itself was on a swivel and mounted on a one-inch plastic mount. All mounts were interchangeable.

TOWER OF DOOM

"This foreboding dark tower was the sinister stronghold of Doctor Doom and his evil henchmen."

This was probably the best piece in the **Secret Wars** series. The tower's 15" x 8" x 6" perimeter

The Freedom Fighter was ready to move out with Iron Man in the Radar Chair and Daredevil in the Gunnery Chair. Captain America, with shield in hand, stands ready for any attack. S. Kimball Collection.

provided villains with three floors of work space. The color of the tower was steel green or dark olive both inside and out. Atop the tower was a revolving observation turret with swivel cannons and a booby trap chair that ejected intruders. By pushing a trigger in the turret, the orange chair flipped back, depositing any intruder sitting there down three flights to the ground.

The second floor was made up of a main control room that held four figures who could look out of a pair of two-inch wide windows. The room was decorated inside with decals and on the outside with mechanical embossings. On the port side of the room was a thin secret door through which most figures could fit.

On the deck outside of the secret door was the end of the elevator/rocket runner. The elevator/rocket was a two-inch square gray platform with a control section jutting up from one side. The control section was a decal with a handle for villains to cling to. The

elevator/rocket was removable and had rocket boosters embossed on the bottom. The elevator/rocket, when attached, could slide down the runner to the ground floor.

The ground floor (from left to right) contained a control station decorated with many decals and a large secret compartment to be opened with a villain's key. To the right of this was a jail-type bar trap door which was triggered from the starboard side of the tower. The bars showed only from the inside of the tower; from the outside, three large horizontal teeth closed in on the entrance, blocking passage. On the far right side of the tower was the control panel which had bright decals on both walls and on the panel itself. The room inverted into the tower, providing depth.

Sliding from a jutting rod connected to the floor above was an orange instrument chair. This enabled the seated **Doctor Doom** to move around the entire first floor.

The Tower of Doom is the fortress for villains like the Magneto, Constrictor, Doctor Doom, and Hobgoblin shown here. Look closely into the windows on the second floor to see Baron Zemo and Kang on watch; also note that the Type 1 Spider-Man is trapped in the jail cell. S. Kimball Collection.

In this Mattel promotional photograph, we see Kang and Doctor Doom in the Doom Chopper hovering over the Type 1 Spider-Man and Captain America in the Turbocopter. Photo courtesy of the J. Main Collection.

Attached to the Tower of Doom were a pair of black two-inch long guns that moved to any number of holes in the sides of the tower or the sliding instrument chair.

TURBO and DOOM CYCLES

Both cycles were from the same mold, with differences only in colors, decals, and the shape of one end of the air cleaner which also doubled as the secret panel key. The cycle mold was 8" x 5" and consisted of a one-piece covered motorcycle with sidecar. The secret panel was located behind the sidecar seat. The main cycle's fairing and canopy were of the same translucent plastic. The fairing tilted forward and the canopy on the sidecar opened, allowing it to carry one action figure.

The main cycle section (without handlebars) held one seated figure with legs behind and arms stretching to the frame. On the front of the fairing were flanking guns which moved forward and back as the vehicle moved forward in a machine gun firing simulation. As the vehicle moved forward, a friction sound was emitted, which was referred to on the box as "Battle Sound."

TURBO and DOOM CHOPPERS

Both Huey-style helicopters were about 16 inches long from the stabilizer blade to the nose of the fuselage. Each came with forward radar antennae on starboard side, a rack of bombs on the port side, forward port side gattling gun, and laser rifle. Two ray guns jutted from the center bottom of the nose.

The cockpits of both choppers seated one figure and the bay in the back held two inside and one on the plank from the bay. The plank was on the port side of the bay with two footholds for the figure. There were two basic helicopter landing skids underneath. There was very little known about these helicopters and none have been reported to us except from the Mattel promotional photograph.

HEROES and VILLAINS MACHINES

Both were six-wheel, two-forward-speed plastic vehicles with all-terrain rubber tires and a three-section articulated frame. There was a lever below the on/off switch for speed, and both vehicles were armed with six weapons. As with the earlier helicopters, none have been reported to us outside of a Mattel catalogue photograph.

DOOM ROLLER

The olive drab-colored Command Unit Vehicle (CUV) propelled a "giant" 10" black plastic wheel. The CUV sat on a three-inch wide perforated track on the inside of the wheel. Outer wheels on the CUV contracted to fit inside the giant wheel's track. The CUV wheels pushed outward to hold the CUV on the track even when upside down. The black wheel, when propelled by the CUV, rolled forward at a quick pace and continued to roll until hitting an obstruction. The Doom Roller continued to back up after it reached an obstacle and then slammed back into the obstruction, usually causing the battery hatch to open, spilling two C-cell batteries!

Attached to the sides of the CUV were flanking gold-painted laser cannons that fell off easily. Atop the CUV was a gold-painted radar key which opened the secret compartment within the cockpit. Inside the cockpit was room for two figures who reclined to an almost horizontal position. Buttons and dials decorated the armrest between the sides of the cockpit and the large, green transparent canopy which clicked securely on to the 7" x 5" CUV.

The front of the CUV had a foam pad with a decal of headlights in a three-over-three-over-one design. On the support struts of either side were decals of three plates with rivets. Under each side was embossed three sets of two trucks and tank-like wheels

Doctor Doom and Magneto (barely visible) are rolling after a fleeing Wolverine while Falcon and Iron Man fly overhead. S. Kimball Collection.

Here we see Wolverine, Captain America (with his Secret Shield), Type 1 Spider-Man, and Iron Man ready for action. S. Kimball Collection.

within. Two one-inch wheels with 1/2" gears attached rotated to drive the giant wheel.

The back of the CUV had, from top to bottom, vent decals, taillight decals, and another set of headlights designed five over one, as well as embossed vents and an escape hatch with rivets. The black wheel was embossed with a heavy tread and no decals.

The **Doom Roller** was sold to merchandisers in standard packs of six. Even in early 1988, the **Doom Roller** was occasionally found in national toy store chains along the East Coast.

STAR DART WITH SPIDER-MAN
and DOOM STAR WITH KANG

A glider armed with laser cannons made up these realistic flying accessories. With a 24" wingspan, the darts had a rubber band-holding seat that fit most figures. The seat rode on an adjustable run which moved for different flight patterns. The dart came with break-away wings that were easily re-assembled after a crash. It was very durable, with a red rubber nose to absorb impact.

SECRET MESSAGES PACK

"Lots of ways to send and receive secret messages."

The message pack was on the usual blister card and came with 16 secret messages for hero and villain shields, one decoder wheel to create a coded message for your favorite character; decode a secret message too, one magic pen with eight sheets of magic paper, instructions and comic adventure story, and one hero shield and one villain shield.

A close-up of Wolverine's removable claws. S. Kimball Collection.

This accessory, which was not used with the figures but with their shields, gave a purpose to the secret shields that came with all accessories. The secret message shield inserts with this pack had

A portion of the black and white comic that came with the Secret Message Pack.

The first set of villains to terrorize the heroes are (left to right) Doctor Doom, Magneto, the many armed Doctor Octopus, and Kang. S. Kimball Collection.

The second series of Super Heroes include (left to right) the Falcon with his pet, Redwing, Daredevil, Type 2 Spider-Man, and the European-released Iceman. S. Kimball Collection.

The second series of super villains include (left to right) the European-released Constrictor, Hobgoblin, Baron Zemo, and the European-released Electro. S. Kimball Collection.

some of the best artwork of the series. The shields in the package already had two very nice picture inserts. One showed **Doctor Doom** climbing into the Doom Roller and when tilted, the Roller seemed to roll off towards the horizon line. The other showed **Captain America** with the Roller in the foreground and when tilted, **Cap** dodged the evil machine.

The instruction sheet showed how to fit the pictures into the shield, how the shield opened secret compartments, and how the decoder and magic pen and paper worked. For example, the coded: "Xq sqw bo," decodes as: "Go for it." The sheet also doubled as a black and white cartoon adventure featuring most of the first issue figures.

The strip started with **Captain America** and **Wolverine** arriving to find **Spider-Man's** Turbo Cycle. After discovering a message in the Cycle's secret compartment and quickly decoding it, the team learned that **Kang** and **Doctor Octopus** had taken **Spidey** to the Tower of Doom. **Captain America** went to get **Iron Man** and **Wolverine** sped to the tower.

At the tower, the wild mutant, **Wolverine**, was discovered and captured by **Doc Octopus** and **Kang**. In the comic, **Doctor Octopus'** tentacles had hooks on the end instead of the grapplers which the actual figure had. **Iron Man** and **Captain America** soon arrived, and in a fight with **Magneto**, caught the "Master of Magnetism" in the tower's trap door. **Iron Man** opened the trap door, **Magneto** slammed into a wall, and the three heroes escaped.

A fight ensued in eleven panels and ended only when **Doctor Octopus** escaped in the rocket/elevator; **Doctor Doom** rolled away in his Doom Roller, threatening revenge; and **Kang** left another Doom Roller in the CUV. Of course **Magneto** remained in the custody of **Spider-Man** and **Captain America**.

The Flying Bat that came with the Hobgoblin figure. Some assembly was required. S. Kimball Collection.

The entire pack was a great buy, even for those who just collected comics, because the adventure story, although unsigned by the artist, had great artwork. This comic was not listed in any comic guide.

LISTINGS

First Series: Early 1984

Blister Pack backs showed **Captain America**, Type 1 **Spider-Man**, **Iron Man**, **Wolverine**, **Doctor Doom**, **Magneto**, **Kang**, and **Doctor Octopus**.

SPIDER-MAN: Type 1; traditional outfit with thin black-painted webbing on costume. Serial No. 7207.

10   25

CAPTAIN AMERICA: Without usual red, white, and blue shield. Serial No. 7205.   **5   10**

IRON MAN: With Type 1 gun. Serial No. 7206.

5   10

WOLVERINE: With two gray "adamtium" claws. Serial No. 7208.   **10   25**

DOCTOR DOOM: Type 2; with Type 1 gun and Type 2 gun. Serial No. 7210.   **3   5**

A close-up of Redwing, the Falcon's mascot.
S. Kimball Collection.

KANG: With purple exoskeleton and Type 1 gun.
Serial No. 7212.   **.50**   **1**

MAGNETO: With Type 1 gun. Serial No. 7211.
                                                         3   **5**

DOCTOR OCTOPUS: With four applied gray tentacles
extending from the waist; grapplers at ends of tentacles.
Serial No. 7213.   **3**   **5**

Second Series: Late 1984

Blister Pack backs showed Type 2 **Spider-Man**,
Daredevil, **Falcon**, **Wolverine**, **Doctor Doom**, **Hobgoblin**,
Baron Zemo, and **Doctor Octopus**.

SPIDER-MAN: Type 2; black and white outfit. Serial
No. 9153.   **10**   **25**

FALCON: Complete with red adjustable wings; Redwing falcon on perch. Serial No. 9141.   **15**   **30**

DAREDEVIL: With gray nightstick. Serial No. 914.
                                                         5   **10**

ICEMAN: Special plastic with marbleized finish; sold
only in Europe. Serial No. 9561.   **25**   **50**

BARON ZEMO: One hand molded in karate chop; Type
1 gun. Serial No. 0139.   **10**   **25**

The back of the Tower of Doom showed a trapped Type
1 Spider-man in the jail cell, Doctor Doom on the sliding command chair, Baron Zemo on watch on the top
floor, and Magneto on the elevator/rocket. Notice that
the orange chair had been triggered. S. Kimball Collection.

HOBGOBLIN: Complete with small orange cape; large
purple flying bat. Serial No. 9138.   **15**   **30**

ELECTRO: Sold only in Europe. Serial No. 9569.
                                                         20   **45**

CONSTRICTOR: Complete with silver whip; frown on
face; sold only in Europe. Serial No. 9631.   **25**   **50**

Accessories

The boxes were all very colorful and carried the Mattel
serial number. Each box contained the appropriate secret
shield and six inserts; all were marked "Safety-Tested-
Conforms to PS 72-76."

FREEDOM FIGHTER: Came unassembled, with black
plastic base, red gunnery chair, blue radar chair, and de-
cals; box top showed Freedom Fighter with Type 1 **Spider-
Man** in the Gunnery Chair, and **Captain America** in the
Radar Chair. The insert photograph showed a child play-
ing with the Fighter and **Captain America** in the Turbo
Copter, Type 1 **Spider-Man** in the Gunnery Chair, and **Iron
Man** in the Radar Chair.

The box for the Star Dart with Spider-Man. S. Kimball Collection.

The Turbo and Doom Cycles are on a collision course with their drivers Wolverine and Doctor Doom. S. Kimball Collection.

Box sides showed five inset photographs of figures in Fighter, close-ups of figures in Gunnery Chair and Radar Chair, Turbo Copter being landed on helipad, and a close-up of the secret compartment in the leg of the Freedom Fighter. Box back was illustrated with Freedom Fighter, Tower of Doom, and the following figures: **Captain America**, Type 1 **Spider-Man**, **Iron Man**, **Wolverine**, **Falcon**, **Daredevil**, **Doctor Doom**, **Doctor Octopus**, **Kang**, **Magneto**, **Baron Zemo**, and **Hobgoblin**. Serial No. 9392.

20　　50

TOWER OF DOOM: Came unassembled, with either steel-green or dark olive-green tower containing removable portions, orange chair, and decals; box top showed Tower of Doom with **Kang** in the turret, **Captain America** in the trap door with **Doctor Doom** standing by with his secret shield. The inset photograph showed a child playing with the tower and **Doctor Doom** in the sliding instrument panel chair. One side of the box was printed with illustrated versions of the photographs on the opposite side. The five inset photographs showed close-ups of figures in

various places in the tower, as well as the secret compartment.

The box back had illustrations of the **Doom Roller**, **Turbo Cycle**, and **Tower of Doom**; as well as **Captain America**, Type 1 **Spider-Man**, **Wolverine**, **Iron Man**, **Doctor Doom**, **Kang**, **Doctor Octopus**, and **Magneto**. Serial No. 7472.

40　　75

TURBO CYCLE: Blue plastic over white. Guns, air cleaner, and sidecar seat were red plastic; yellow "TURBO" decal outlined in red on side of sidecar. Front of box had clear window pack and lettering only. The back of the box showed a photo of the unmanned cycle. The following figures were also shown: **Captain America**, Type 1 **Spider-Man**, **Iron Man**, **Wolverine**, **Doctor Doom**, **Kang**, **Doctor Octopus**, and **Magneto**. The box bottom showed a photo of the unmanned cycle. Serial No. 7473.

15　　30

DOOM CYCLE: Purple plastic over black; guns, air cleaner, and sidecar seat were gray; yellow, orange, and red flames decal on side of sidecar. Front of box had clear window pack and lettering only; the back showed a photo

Here we see the two types of Spider-Man costumes, (left, Type 1; right, Type 2). S. Kimball Collection.

This was how Kang (left) and the Type 2 Spider-Man (right) came with their respective flying darts. Notice the shield inserts in the bags. S. Kimball Collection.

of the unmanned cycle. The following figures were also shown: **Captain America**, Type 1 **Spider-Man**, **Iron Man**, **Wolverine**, **Doctor Doom**, **Kang**, **Doctor Octopus**, and **Magneto**. The box bottom showed a photo of the unmanned cycle. Serial No. 7600.   **15**   **30**

TURBO COPTER: This vehicle was blue with decals on the top of the cab and the numbered decal "234" on the stabilizer. There was a red, white, and blue star on the tail and the same star on the nose. Decals on prop edges and in cockpit. Box information unknown. Serial No. 9246.   **40**   **75**

DOOM CHOPPER: Metallic green vehicle with same decals on top of cab as as were on Turbo Copter. "532" was the decal on the stabilizer and it is unknown as to what the decal was on the tail. A portrait of **Doctor Doom** was on the nose. Decals on prop edges and in cockpit. Box information unknown. Serial No. 9572.   **40**   **75**

MARVEL SUPER HEROES MACHINE: Figure sat low and forward with a control panel in front and a wraparound cushion to hold the figure in place. Behind the figure was a white wing with two sets of flanking missiles and one flanking below the wing; other colors unknown. Box information unknown. Serial No. 9877.   **50**   **100**

MARVEL SUPER VILLAINS MACHINE: Figure sat above and centered on the body, two missiles flanked either side of chair on the wing-type platform; radar dish was to the right of the figure, colors unknown. Box information unknown. Serial No. 9880.   **50**   **100**

STAR DART: Large white flying wing came with Type 2 **Spider-Man**; had red seat, skeleton, and nose; black laser cannons; and red, white, blue, and black decals.

Box top showed dart with Type 2 **Spider-Man** and inset of child launching dart. Box back showed the same photo as top; also photos of Freedom Fighter with Type 1 **Spider-Man** and **Iron Man**, and the following figures: **Captain America**, **Iron Man**, **Falcon**, **Wolverine**, Type 2 **Spider-Man**, **Doctor Doom**, **Kang**, **Doctor Octopus**, **Baron**

The CUV apart from the Doom Roller. S. Kimball Collection.

Zemo, and **Hobgoblin**. Box back also stated the fact that there were more Super Heroes. Serial No. 9693.
   40   **80**

DARK STAR: Large black flying wing came with **Kang** figure; had silver seat, skeleton, and nose; red laser cannons; and red and magenta decals.

Box top showed dart with **Kang** and inset of child launching dart. Box back showed the same photo as top; also photos of Freedom Fighter with Type 1 **Spider-Man** and **Iron Man**, and the following figures: **Captain America**, **Iron Man**, **Falcon**, **Wolverine**, Type 2 **Spider-Man**, **Doctor Doom**, **Kang**, **Doctor Octopus**, **Baron Zemo**, and **Hobgoblin**. Serial No. 9692.   **15**   **30**

DOOM ROLLER: Olive-drab Command Unit Vehicle came unassembled; with black plastic wheel, gold-painted laser cannons, various removable portions, no decals, required two C-cell batteries. Box top showed unmanned CUV in Roller. The inset photograph showed a close-up of the separate unmanned CUV. All photos on this box contained a version of the Doom Roller with a clear cockpit, instead of the gray cover that actually came with the CUV.

Box sides showed insert photographs or illustration of the unmanned roller, open unmanned cockpit, separate unmanned CUV, chrome radar key with **Magneto** and **Doctor Doom** in the open cockpit. Box back showed illustrations of **Turbo Cycle**, **Tower of Doom**, and **Doom Roller**. Figures illustrated were of **Captain America**, Type 1 **Spider-Man**, **Wolverine**, **Iron Man**, **Doctor Doom**, **Kang**, **Doctor Octopus**, and **Magneto**. Serial No. 7474.   **25**   **50**

SECRET MESSAGES PACK: As described in text, blister pack was the same as the figures and the back was also identical to that of the first issue. Serial No. 7599.   **25**   **50**

All of these items carry the Secret Wars logo. Each item is listed below and has a corresponding number in the illustration at right. S. Kimball Collection and illustration.

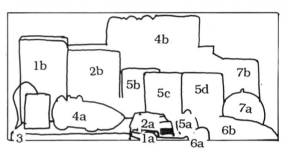

MORE SECRET WARS COLLECTIBLES

When a theme is destined to be a successful marketing idea, as was the case with the Marvel **Secret Wars** concept, many manufacturers will jump on the merchandising bandwagon. **Secret Wars** action figures are but the tip of the iceberg in terms of the licensing value of Marvel Comics characters. Following is a partial list of toys and products licensed by Marvel. These items, while not action figures strictly speaking, are based on action figures, and, therefore, deserve our consideration.

Both **Super Powers** and **Defenders of the Earth** had their share of other licensed items. The **Secret Wars** licensed products represented only a few of the major comic characters. Except for the Mattel action figures and accessories, only **Captain America**, **Spider-Man**, and **Doctor Doom** appeared in mass-merchandised goods. There were exceptions, such as **Doctor Octopus** in a pocket-sized bubble gum dispenser.

Please note that the items discussed here are **Secret Wars** products and not **Marvel Super Heroes**. It seems that before and after the **Secret Wars**, most of the Marvel-licensed toys and products carried the **Marvel Super Heroes** name. Those items should not be included in the **Secret Wars** collection because they do not carry the three-dimensional logo: "SECRET WARS." Another **Secret Wars** item that is listed below but is not included in the color photograph is the **Secret Wars** T-shirt worn by the author in his photograph.

LISTINGS

(1a) SECRET WARS CAPTAIN AMERICA DIGITAL QUARTZ WATCH: 1984; blue watch with **Captain America** shield. 10 20

(1b) Similar to **(1a)**, but with **Doctor Doom** face. 10 20

(2a) SECRET WARS SPIDER-VAN: Buddy-L, 1985; one of four vehicles in set. **(2b)** was a box containing Spider-cycle, Spider-copter, and Spider-buggy. 15 30

(3) SECRET WARS PRESTO MAGIX RUB-ONS: 1986; included rub-ons of many Secret Wars figures and accessories. 5 10

(4a) SECRET WARS SPIDER-MAN REMOTE CONTROL RACER: 1984; racer connected to control via black cable. Racer ran forward and turned left in reverse. **(4b)** was box for **Spider-Man** racer. Other racers included **Captain America**, **Rocket Racer**, and **Doctor Doom Dragster Racer**. 15 30

(5a) SECRET WARS SPIDER-MAN POCKET GUM-BALL DISPENSERS: 1985; red and blue with **Spider-Man** figure. Each figure had articulated arm which, when raised, allowed access to gumball pouch. **5** **10**

(5b) Similar to **(5a)**, but featured **Captain America**. **5** **10**

(5c) Similar to **(5a)**, but featured **Doctor Doom**. **5** **10**

(5d) Similar to **(5a)**, but featured **Doctor Octopus**. **5** **10**

(6a) SECRET WARS BALLOON: 1985; orange balloon with **Wolverine/Doctor Doom** illustrated. Other balloons included **Captain America/Spider-Man**. **(6b)** was a pack of balloons. Price for pack of balloons: **3** **7**

(7a) SECRET WARS SPIDER-MAN AM RADIO: 1986; AM radio in the shape of **Spider-Man's** face. **(7b)** was box for radio. **8** **15**

SECRET WARS T-SHIRT: 1984-86; many types of T-shirts can be found. The two that the author has seen are listed.

(A) Black with only **Secret Wars** logo over chest. **10** **15**

(B) Light blue with battling figures and **Secret Wars** logo. **10** **15**

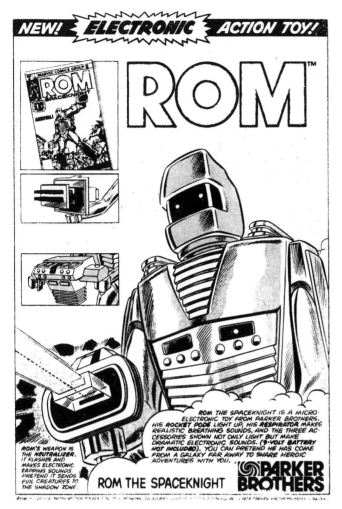

This advertisement from a 1978 Marvel Comic advertisement shows the coming of ROM from the toy shelves to the comics. Copyright 1978 Marvel Comics. S. Kimball Collection.

FROM TOYS TO COMICS

*How to Merchandise
and make it readable*

Recently, comic book readers have become discontented, even agitated, by the influx of toys and toy-related cartoons appearing in comic books. These readers do not think that the toys are interesting or appropriate comic book material. What they do not realize is that comic book publishers have chosen to promote toy-related stories because the comic book is such an effective advertising medium for characters. One example is **G. I. Joe**. This toy has been incorporated into three popular comic book series

and a magazine, not to mention the very successful television series. However, not all toys translate into successful comic book characters; some of these unfortunates have been **Defenders of the Earth**, **Mad Balls**, and **Captain Action** comic books.

The toy-to-comic concept seems to have begun in 1967, when DC Comics designed a comic book based on the **Captain Action** toy. The comic featured accessories and other figures, although **Captain Ac-**

tion rarely changed his original outfit. Although unsuccessful at the time of its original publication, the five-issue series is now highly desirable among comic book collectors.

It was not until 1975 that the toy-to-comic idea reappeared. Mego toys produced the **Micronauts**, the first toy to successfully become a comic book. With over 40 issues in the first comic, and 24 in the second, these comics were well written and beautifully drawn. The toys were of similar quality, with Hard plastic features and metal-riveted articulation. These features were so popular that today it is difficult to find an action figure without similar construction.

When Mego toys ended production of the **Micronauts**, it seemed to give Marvel Comics the nod to expand their version of the "Microverse." The **Micronauts** reappeared with Marvel Comics' most popular **Super Hero** team, the **X-Men**, in a two-issue limited series. This combination so increased the **Micronauts'** popularity that another series was created. Unfortunately, this comic books' appeal ebbed, too, and the second series ended with the death of all the major characters.

In the late 1970s, Ideal Toys marketed its popular **ROM, Spacenight**. Although the comic series lasted for only a short fifty-issue run, almost every major Marvel character, from **Captain America** to the **X-Men**, made an appearance at one time or another. Even after **ROM, Spacenight** had stopped being published, his arch enemies, the **Dire Wraiths**, lived on in other comics. The popularity of the toy version, however, lasted only a single year. (More about **ROM** will be found in a later volume of **Super Hero Toys**.)

Shown are the five issues of the Captain Action comic book series published by DC Comics. S. Baum Collection. Copyright 1967/1988 DC Comics. All Rights Reserved.

The toy-to-comic has been successful in the 1980s. The most popular has been **He-Man and the Masters of the Universe**. Others have included the **Air Raiders**, **Captain Power and the Soldiers of the Future**, **Defenders of the Earth**, **G. I. Joe: the Real American Hero**, **Inhumanoids**, **M. A. S. K.**, **Mad Balls**, **Robotech**, the **Real Ghostbusters**, **Silverhawks**, **She-Ra: Princess of Power**, **Supernaturals**, **Thundercats**, **Tigersharks**, **Transformers**, **Visionaries**, **Voltron**, and the **Wheeled Warriors**. All of these toy-to-comics were also TV cartoons. Though, in 1988, the majority of these toys are still on the toy shelves and many of the comics yet on the magazine racks, these faddish, child-directed characters are not likely to have any real longevity in the marketplace. One exception to this may be the **Transformers**, whose toys and Marvel comic books have rung up high sales for the past three years.

REVERSE LICENSING

Selling the toy during the show,
or...
The half-hour commercial

Licensing means permission. To license a product is to formally rent a trademark or copyright material from its owner for use on merchandise. Thus, in the world of comics, for example, a well-known character like **Superman**, who was created for young boys' reading entertainment, winds up on T-shirts, coffee mugs, and the like. This wedding between character and salable product often proves to be not only a financial boon for the product manufacturer, but also may increase the popularity of the original character. This often continues in a circular manner, in which the character boosts the product, which boosts the character, which further boosts the product, and so on.

In the last five years, a new twist has developed in the venerable cartoon character licensing game. Where, traditionally, first some cartoon character would make its appearance, establish its popularity, and later spawn a line of toys, there has been a recent trend towards "reverse licensing." In this topsy-turvy situation, the toy is created first, and only later is a comic book or cartoon program developed. The importance of these programs is not necessarily their entertainment value, but the ability they have to boost the sales of the line of toys.

This trend found its beginnings when Mattel Toys sank seven million into the production of the **He-Man** cartoon show in order to promote its new line of toys. By the end of the year, the licensed merchandise produced by Mattel, mainly action figures, saw their

This comic book advertisement was another illustrated tool in marketing Captain Action and can be found in Issue No. 2 of the 1967 DC Captain Action series. S. Baum Collection. Copyright 1967/1988 DC Comics. All Rights Reserved.

sales triple. By 1984, many similar programs promoting copycat toys had been produced.

A **Wall Street Journal** report showed that 24 out of the 35 cartoon programs on the air in 1987 had toy tie-ins. Some say the statistic seems to support the criticism that toy-based cartoons are little more than expanded commericals. Recently, parents began to exclaim against the toy/TV tie-in, and according to the Journal's report, "The toy industry imitated itself off the air." A similar report in a late 1987 issue of the **Comic Buyer's Guide**, in discussing the comic book connection to all this, indicated that cartoons were released only a week before the comic, and the comic was released two weeks before the action figures!

It is estimated that a toy company spends five years building a new product idea, even knowing that the period of the toy's high popularity will last only a year, and may produce just enough sales to cover its research and development. Thus, strong promotional techniques become the companies' life-lines for their short-lived products.

On the other hand, certain characters, and their licensed spin-offs, seem destined to last forever, including some Super Heroes: **Superman**, **Spider-Man**, **Batman**, and **Captain America**, and others. DC Comics' characters are currently licensed by seventy-five different companies. In 1978, when the first **Superman** movie was released, 140 companies showed interest in the licensing, and over 500 different products were manufactured.

In summary, of the $60 billion in 1977 retail sales of licensed toys, only $7.8 billion was generated by the toy industry alone. The obvious reason behind licensing is, like most things in these times, to make money... and it makes lots of money. Not that it is a bad thing to do... unless, of course, licensed products cheapen the quality of their symbiotic host.

Manufactured from 1984 through 1986, the Super Powers Collection included 33 figures which sold in many toy and department stores throughout the United States and Canada. In this photograph, which shows the planet, Apokolips, we see the battle of Good and Evil. From left to right are the evil Lex Luthor, Kalibak, Steppenwolf, Mr. Freeze, Desaad, Darkseid (on top of rock), and Orion. On the side of good are Batman, Wonder Woman, Cyborg, and Hawkman. Flying overhead are Dr. Fate and Superman in the Supermobile, as a rocket fires from Kalibak's Boulder Bomber. The painted backdrop illustrates the Darkseid Tower of Darkness which was never mass-produced. S. Kimball Collection.

SUPER POWERS COLLECTION

A Decision of Character

With the Assistance of Jim Carlo

"The greatest heroes the world has ever known versus the meanest villains the world has ever feared. Characters known and loved by millions of kids and collectors alike. The most powerful heroes and dastardly villains from all corners of the universe brought to action figure form like never before!"

From the pages of DC Comics and manufactured by Kenner (now Kenner-Parker) Toys: **THE SUPER POWERS COLLECTION**.

Issued in three types of blister card packages, each figure, ranging in size from 4" tall (**Penguin**) to 5-3/4" tall (**Darkseid**) was jointed at the arms, hips, and knees, and had a turnable head. Most came with a 2-3/4" x 4-1/4" mini-comic book describing the adventures of that particular character. Also featured was a cut-out 2-3/4" x 4-1/2" collector card on the back of each package which contained information about each character. This information included secret identity, powers, weaknesses, and enemies. On the opposite side of the card was a picture of the particular character. (1986 figures did not have pictures on their collector card, nor did they have mini-comic books inside.)

Each of the **Super Powers** figures came equipped with "power action" which corresponded to each character's power. For instance, when **Aquaman's** arms were squeezed together, his power action deep sea kicking legs were activated; when **Hawkman's** legs were squeezed together, his power action flight wings flapped; **Brainiac** kicked; **Flash** ran, etc...

Kenner Toys, in conjunction with DC Comics, produced quality action figures that were superb representations of the characters. The staff at Kenner and DC did their homework in designing the molds for these figures. With such good design and high quality, why did production continue for only three years, from 1984 through 1986?

One reason collectors feel that the **Super Powers** line did not last, was Kenner's method of packaging figures. Merchandisers received only 24 assorted characters to the carton which was not a large enough assortment. More often than not, big name toy chains opened boxes, supposedly containing 24 assorted figures, and only found three or four different figures with up to 18 of a single figure. Obviously, if the figures were packaged in groups of six different characters (four of each), it would have given the merchandiser a wider variety for better sales.

Because of this haphazard distribution method, certain characters were in abundance and others hard to find, depending on which toy store got what selection of figures. Many East Coast collectors experienced difficulty obtaining the **Penguin** during 1984, **Desaad** in 1985, and **Cyborg** in 1986. However, in 1988, it is still possible to walk into certain toy stores and find large stacks of **Darkseids**.

By late 1985, consumer enthusiasm had waned and subsequently the number of orders placed by retailers to Kenner declined.

In the Batcave, we see Batman at the computer, Wonder Woman with her golden lasso around the Joker, and the Penguin. Robin is assessing the situation from the Batmobile. These figures are from the first series of Super Powers action figures. S. Kimball Collection. The Batcave is not part of the Super Powers collection, but was built by the author.

On the rooftops overlooking Gotham City, we see Hawkman, Flash, Green Lantern, and Superman, preparing to capture Brainiac and Lex Luthor. Aquaman is standing on the outside of the Delta Probe One which hovers over the scene. All of these figures are from the first series of Super Powers figures. S. Kimball Collection.

Some collectors blame DC Comics for the discontinuation of the action figures. Unlike Marvel Comics' **Secret Wars** mini-series, which ran at about the same time as DC's **Super Powers** series and involved only their major characters, **Super Powers** brought in many new, unheard of Heroes (e.g. **Golden Pharoah**). They failed to spark any real enthusiasm in collectors, and seemed to have been created just for the purpose of offering a more diverse selection of action figures.

The consensus among collectors is that Kenner would have had greater success if more women figures had been included, such as **Supergirl**, **Batgirl**, or **Catwoman**, instead of just **Wonder Woman**. However, boys between the ages of six and twelve make up eighty percent of the Super Hero comic-buying public, and boys of that age would much rather have all male figures than (yucky) girl figures! Perhaps it was realized that to build up a female Super Hero market, a much greater investment risk would have to be made in order to encroach upon the large and always growing selection of dolls which girls already enjoyed.

Some of the recent new "stars" of DC's main line of comics, such as the **Blue Beetle** and **Nightwing**, would have also sold well, also. More traditional villain figures, such as **the Riddler**, **Sinestro**, **Mr. Mxyzptlk**, or **Bizarro**, would probably have been a hit, too. And a special offer such as "Buy **Superboy** and send in for a free **Krypto**" would have been a wonderful and successful offer.

In the vein of accessories, the **Fortress of Solitude**, the **Batcave**, or the **Guardian's Citadell** (with several small **Guardians** included) would have been welcome additions to the already fantastic list of accessories.

Once the **Super Powers** line was discontinued, the majority of leftover stock was bought by discount stores (i.e., K mart, Ames, Woolworths, etc.). During the close-out period, it was possible to purchase the figures for as little as $1. These low prices were immediately met with great enthusiasm. The most desirable figures sold quickly, while a huge stock of unpopular figures remained. Certain accessories, too, were and still are available, such as the **Kaibak Boulder Bomber** and the **Lex-Soar 7**.

Now that the rush has subsided with most of the figures in collectors' hands, the value of the figures has begun to increase. And so, the **Super Powers** collection seems destined to become desirable collectibles far into the future. Despite the unpopularity of some characters, the detail on all the figures is impressive, as is the hand-painted look and authentic colors. It is this kind of quality that keeps the collection in the forefront of action figures.

FIGURES

The figures from the **Super Powers Collection** were all dressed in their traditional costumes, some

of which date to the 1930s. The first series of **Super Powers** figures was comprised of some of DC's most popular Super Heroes. This included **Superman**, **Batman**, **Aquaman**, **Robin**, **Wonder Woman**, **Flash**, **Green Lantern**, and **Hawkman**. Some figures came with accessories, such as **Hawkman** with a club and **Wonder Woman** with her golden lasso.

The villainous side of the first issue was represented by the evil **Lex Luthor**, **Joker**, **Brainiac**, and **Penguin**. **Lex Luthor** wore a special suit of armor that was especially made for both the action figures and the comics. **Luthor's** symbol can be found in the glossary section at the end of this book.

The second **Super Powers** series presented some of the less mainstream Super Heroes and villains along with a few old regulars. Heroes included the **Martian Manhunter**, **Green Arrow**, **Red Tornado**, **Firestorm**, and **Doctor Fate**. They were soon followed by the evil **Darkseid**, **Kalibak**, **Mantis**,

Fire Storm, Doctor Fate, Martian Manhunter, and Red Tornado fly to the rescue of Green Arrow who is in the Justice Jogger. The Jogger is surrounded by the villains of Apokolips: Kalibak, Parademon, Steppenwolf, and their leader, Darkseid. These characters made up the second series of Super Powers figures. S. Kimball Collection.

The villainous Mr. Freeze puts his hands up and pleads no contest to Captain Marvel (SHAZAM!), the Golden Pharoah, Cyborg, Samari, and Plastic Man. These figures are part of the the third Super Powers series of action figures. S. Kimball Collection.

Parademon, and **Steppenwolf**. All of the villains were relatively new to DC Comics as compared to the first series villains whose origins go back to the 1940s and 50s.

The third series of **Super Powers** took a sales "nose dive." It seems that **Super Powers'** popularity had worn thin. Third series heroes included **Captain Marvel (SHAZAM!)**, **Mister Miracle**, **Plasticman**, **Samari**, **Golden Pharoah**, **Cyclotron**, and **Cyborg**. Except for **Robin** (first series), **Cyborg** was the only member of the **Teen Titans** seen in **Super Powers** action figure form. Third series villains included: **Orion**, **Tyr**, and **Mr. Freeze**. As you can tell, the heroes outnumbered the villains. **Orion** has been listed as a villain because of his schizophrenic personality.

The only other figure not listed in any of the series was **Clark Kent**, who we all know is **Superman's** alter ego. This figure was a mail-order giveaway or could be ordered from Sears. It is described later in this chapter.

VEHICLES AND ACCESSORIES

BATCOPTER

The blue and black plastic Batcopter somewhat resembled the Batcopter from the comic books, but in no way resembled the Batcopter of the 1960's "BATMAN!" TV series. It was also basically inaccurate in size when compared to the Mattel **Secret Wars** helicopters. Unfortunately, the orange translucent cockpit cover permitted room for only one action figure in the cockpit. The cockpit was decorated with multicolored decals.

Flanking black wings each had a Batsymbol and acted as landing gear (sleds). A matching black-winged stabilizer was screwed to the back of the fuselage. On the nose of the fuselage was a black dart tip with two yellow triangular eye decals on the

Mr. Freeze is caught in the Batmobile's crook catcher as Robin looks on. Notice that Batman holds Mr. Freeze's temperature-control helmet. S. Kimball Collection.

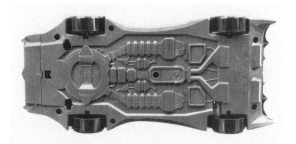

The detailed underside of the Batmobile. Notice the simulated Hoverfan.

In the Batcave we see the Batmobile with its occupants, Batman and Robin. Notice that the two eye-lights are up. S. Kimball Collection.

As Batman hovers the Batcopter over the rooftops of Gotham City, Robin dangles on the dart tip. S. Kimball Collection.

top side. A cable was attached from the dart tip to the inside of the nose, which had a manual winch knob that was turned in order to retract the cable. A button under the nose released the dart tip and launched it to the full end of the cable.

The rotor shaft supported three rotor blades above the copter and was connected to a villain grabber. The rotor was also turned manually.

BATMOBILE

Over 10 inches long, this vehicle is more reminiscent of the Batmobile of the comics rather than that from the 1960's TV show. It could seat two figures and had three different activating mechanisms as well as a friction-powered sound motor which was activated by pushing the vehicle.

The windshield of orange translucent plastic, similar to Batcopter's windshield (described below),

protected the Dynamic Duo from the weather, and many decals decorated the inside of the cockpit. The Batsymbols decorated both doors, which were embossed and did not open.

The Batmobile was equipped with three action features. The headlights were triggered from the inside of the vehicle, as were all three mechanisms. The Batmobile also featured a battering ram that, when triggered, elongated a full two inches. Another button released the crook catcher claw that instantly snapped around a crook from the rear of the vehicle.

SUPERMOBILE

Protecting **Superman** from the Kryptonite crystal (see Lex-Soar 7) which **Lex Luthor** carried was the blue Supermobile with a red translucent windshield.

The Supermobile had a button atop one of the dorsal fins that activated a gray, jagged battering ram that extended about one inch. The cockpit seated only one figure.

DELTA PROBE ONE

Of all the **Super Powers** vehicles, the Delta Probe One was the most imaginative. There was virtually no assembly required for this eight-inch vehicle. The craft consisted of a large globe-shaped cockpit with delta-shaped wings extending vertically from the back end.

The cockpit consisted of a red, transparent plastic globe with a tilt-down windshield (about half the size of the globe). By rotating one or both of the accompanying blue side guns, the windshield would slide down and lock with a "click." In order to fit a figure into the craft, the inner cockpit was rotated by twisting the blue radar dish on the underside by half a turn.

Once the figure was in a seated position, back facing you, you once again gave the radar dish a half turn to point the cockpit towards you. A blue trigger release to close the windshield was located on the underside of the craft's nose.

There were two more blue guns on a removable turret atop the vehicle which followed the front sight of the figure in the cockpit.

At the rear of the craft were the villain cover and villain restraints. The villain cover was made of the same material as the cockpit's windshield and swung down to cover the head and torso of the trapped villain. The villain restraints were two panels of red plastic that, when triggered, closed around the villain, locking him there.

Underneath the rear of the vehicle was a bomb bay that held a 1-1/2" light blue plastic bomb. A small, blue plastic lever released the bomb.

The overall appearance of the Delta Probe One resembled a 1950's-style bathysphere, which would lead you to believe that **Aquaman** might pilot the vehicle. But all the illustrations and box photos showed **Robin** as the pilot.

JUSTICE JOGGER

The red Justice Jogger vehicle was intended to aid the non-flying Super Hero who had to travel the unpredictable terrain of Apokolips.

The windup Jogger had a blue clockwork key that was disguised as a radar antenna, which, when wound, "jogged" the seated figure some ten feet. The vehicle was comprised of an enclosed red chair with decals; a yellow transparent canopy that covered half of the figure; and a yellow control bar that swung

Superman alongside the Supermobile.

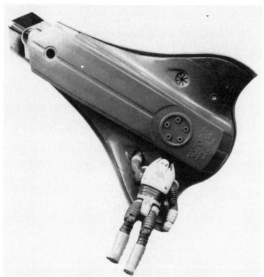

The underside of the Supermobile spacecraft showed two crook wrist-grabbers that held one figure each. The battering ram is extended.

The Joker is seen here trapped in the villain restraints with the villain cover up. S. Kimball Collection.

down to become a step and then closed in on the figure, locking him securely to the chair.

SUPER POWERS VEHICLE

According to the entry in the Sears Wish Book for 1985, this **"Super Powers** vehicle has a motorized roaring sound and 2 movable machine guns. Steer-

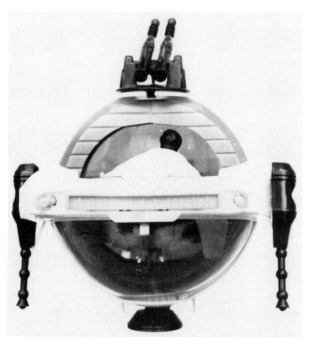

The Delta Probe One and the back of its seemingly unlikely pilot, Robin. Note that in order to place a figure inside the cockpit, he must be bent into a sitting position and placed in backwards. S. Kimball Collection.

ing wheel flips to right or left side." Reader input needed.

ALL TERRAIN TRAPPER

Shown in some **Super Powers** mini-catalogues, its exact details are not known. The vehicle resembled the Lunar Bubble from the **Major Matt Mason** series by Mattel in the late 1960s. The object was to trap a villain in this bubble and transport him to the Hall of Justice. Reader input needed.

HALL OF JUSTICE PLAYSET

The Kenner/DC team put a lot of creative effort into the design of the **Super Powers** accessories, but

The small blue bomb located in the bomb bay is triggered by the accompanying lever. S. Kimball Collection.

The Computer Command Center contained a large computer console, monitor screens, rejuvenation equipment, and an elevator to the roof. S. Kimball Collection.

the crowning jewel (and the author's personal favorite) was the Hall of Justice Playset.

As with all the accessories in the **Super Powers** collection, the Hall was molded in brightly-colored plastic and decorated with multicolored decals. When extended, the two-piece front of the yellow plastic structure was 34" long and 10-1/2" tall at the apex of the centered arch. The blue plastic wall which extended from the center of the front into the playset divided the Hall into two rooms: a jail and a computer command center.

The Jail: The left side of the structure could hold up to six villains in five separate compartments with either decorated bars or guard straps to restrain them. On the far left of the jail room were two cells, one with a red guard strap and one with a red swinging door of bars. Above the cells was a section with a purple decal with red-lettered "NUTRALIZER" printed on it.

Centered over the top middle jail section was a yellow trap door on a blue ceiling/floor. It was equipped with a yellow underside latch which, when turned, dropped one end of the door into the center two-villain holding cell. This cell had two large red swinging doors of bars. The backdrop to this cell and the backside of the front arch above it was a brightly il-

lustrated lithographed cardboard sheet. The inside of the arch had a gold illustration of "blind justice" over a backdrop of red and white vertical stripes. The walls from the ceiling of the holding cell to the floor were illustrated with lines and blocks of gray descending in perspective to illustrate depth. A red plastic bench was attached to the sides of the cell to seat the villains.

To the right of the large holding cell were two cells, one with a red swinging door of bars and the other with a red guard strap. Above the cells was a section with a yellow- and red-striped decal with green-lettered "KRYPTONITE VAULT" printed on it.

As you "turned the corner" and saw the blue wall, you would first notice nine decals depicting symbols for **Superman**, **Wonder Woman**, **Batman**, **Flash**, **Green Lantern**, **Aquaman**, **Robin**, and **Hawkman**. A center sticker depicted the **Super Powers** Collection logo. The far right of the wall was embossed with the words, "ON DUTY," and had a set of vertical and horizontal slots with covers to attach the various hero's comic book data files.

In the center of the wall were two yellow doors, embossed to resemble various thicknesses of armament. Through the doors lay the most colorful area of the Hall, the Computer Command Center.

The Delta Probe One rests on the landing pad as Superman stands by. The Red Tornado heads toward the elevator to the main room. S. Kimball Collection.

To the far left of the Command Center's blue, middle wall, was a red elevator with yellow floor which led to the roof. The elevator could hold only one figure at a time. However, large figures, such as **Darkseid**, **Kalibak**, and **Hawkman**, could not fit.

To the right of the yellow doors (which on the Command Center side had a small decal each, at doorknob height) was a recessed area with a set of

twelve various-sized, colorful, decaled monitor screens and five decaled clocks for various cities. The clocks were frozen at the following times:

- 5:50 in Metropolis (**Superman's** home town).
- 3:10 in "Gothem" City (**Batman** and **Robin's** turf, also note the misspelling of Gotham).
- 4:45 in Atlantis (**Aquaman's** kingdom).
- 7:16 in Thanagor (**Hawkman's** hidden city).
- 11:12 in Midway City (**Flash** hailed from here).

On the front wall of the Computer Console area were two sets of two one-figure transporters which flanked a cardboard lithograph of what appeared to be generators. The lithograph, as was the Jail's inside, was illustrated with perspective lines to give a feeling of depth. Each set of transporters shared one red guard strap which had a centered round decal with the word "TRANSPORTER" lithographed on it.

Above the left transporters was a separate area marked with an orange rectangular decal which read, "REJUVENATION CENTER" in red letters. Above the right set was another separate area with a blue rectangular decal which read "AQUATIC POOL" in white letters. This was obviously for **Aquaman**.

The red plastic computer console swung down from the recessed "generator" room and rested on a blue floor. To one side were four seats embossed to

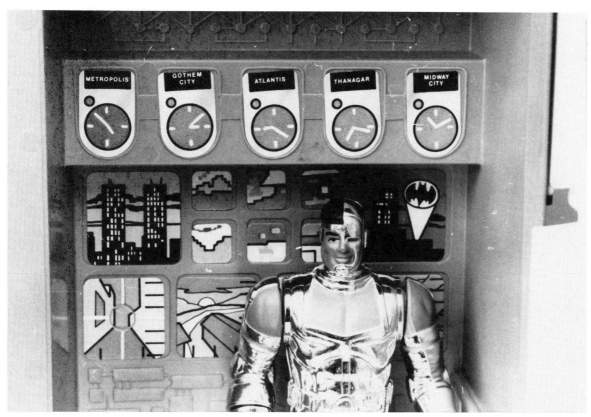

Five clocks tell the time in various cities in the Super Powers universe. Note the misspelling of the word, "Gothem." S. Kimball Collection.

resemble leather. The back of each was decaled. The console itself had various decals of monitors and key-punch cards, as well as embossed buttons and dials. On the base of the console were two more brightly-colored decals. The console top was removable from the swinging base and underneath the base was yet another illustrated cardboard panel.

Landing Pad: The landing pad straddled the three walls of the Hall with stabilizing plastic tabs. The red pad was eight inches in diameter and was also laden with decals. The pad was large enough to hold any of the **Super Powers** vehicles including the monsterous **Darkseid** Destroyer.

In all, the "Golden" Hall of Justice made a great playset for the **Super Powers** figures and accessories, and had room for just about all the figures. Though the outside was not accurate in proportion to the size of the figures, it did have beautiful artwork. The arch was outlined in red and elaborated with various leading lines, as well as a few decals. The outside back of the Hall had a stirring embossment of the four main (and probably the most notable) **Super Powers** figures: **Superman**, **Batman**, **Wonder Woman**, and **Robin**.

The Hall latched together with four yellow, pliable latches that were easily pushed together and pulled apart. The whole Hall folded unto itself, forming a box complete with handle for easy carrying.

The Hall of Justice folded together. Notice the handle. S. Kimball Collection.

LEX SOAR 7

Lex Luthor's ship, the Lex-Soar 7, was a nice piece of plastic work. It had a cream and purple body that slightly resembled an F-18 with a flattened cockpit and nose. It had two side-mounted cannons.

The green translucent cockpit cover swung up and down and locked to the fuselage. Inside the cockpit were two attached power cables that connected to **Lex Luthor's** ultra suit. Behind the cockpit section, but in front of the wings, was a Kryptonite vault, com-

The Jail portion of the Hall of Justice had five holding cells to accommodate six villains. S. Kimball Collection.

From the chamber at the rear of the Lex-Soar 7, Lex Luthor has pulled out the Kryptonite which he now holds over a defeated Superman. S. Kimball Collection.

plete with a crystal of Kryptonite. Underneath the landing gear were two gripping claw-like vises. They were activated by squeezing the two dorsals together.

DARKSEID DESTROYER

This, the largest of the vehicles and the flagship of **Darkseid's** fleet, was really six vehicles in one. The large main ship was an ominous purple color, and had a gun/cannon flanking the nose. Decals (which were quite difficult to apply) decorated the ship's exterior and the inside of the purple cockpit. The only entrance into the cockpit was from the rear, and only the throne portion fit inside.

As shown in the accompanying photograph, the two triceptors could be detached from the wings of the Destroyer and attached to the throne or to each other, which made two separate types of vehicles. The throne itself was a vehicle. The Destroyer's wings could be moved to six different heights via the lever on the back of the throne section. But, when the wings were up, the Destroyer was not very stable and could be easily knocked over.

Making up a portion of the landing gear was a trigger. This trigger activated a hideous screeching "electronic" noise and, when the throne was attached, lit up the entire cockpit as well as **Darkseid's** eyes.

KALIBAK BOULDER BOMBER

The ugly **Kalibak** Boulder Bomber was the most "cartoony" of the vehicles. Its olive-drab colors gave it a rugged appearance, while its thrashing red "teeth" twisted back and forth when the vehicle was rolled forward. It made a sound similar to that of the Batmobile.

The Boulder Bomber had one lethal quality...its arsenal. Two top launchers propelled red missiles some fifteen feet with a fairly hard impact. The Boulder Catapult delivered a hard, yet hollow, boulder to targets at a range of twenty feet or more.

TOWER OF DARKNESS

This playset, equal in size but not complexity to the Hall of Justice, was a wonder to behold. For everything that the Hall of Justice held in bright colors, the Tower of Darkness trapped in dark, ominous purples, blues, grays, and blacks. Interestingly, although some collectors say that they have seen this fortress, others say that it was never manufactured. The accompanying photograph was from the mini-catalogue found in some of the other accessory boxes.

The playset was molded in **Darkseid's** image complete with shoulders, arms, and flexing hands which served as a grabbing trap. The contents included:

Omega effect eyes.

Two rotating cannons that made a clicking sound.

A revolving front gate that turned into a jail cell.

A rotating body vice.

A head-slamming elevator.

A capture-jaw that chomped down on its captive and then dropped the victim into the lava pit below.

A trap door that opened into a spiked pit.

MAIL-IN OFFERS

• **Free Color Poster**: featured all 12 first-year figure characters. The poster measured 18" x 24" and could be ordered with two proof-of-purchase seals from any of the Kenner **Super Powers** toys. There were also two different posters that were found in assorted accessory boxes. They were also available through retail and specialty comic book stores.

The illuminating, evil-shaped Darkseid Destroyer with Darkseid approaching the cockpit, as a host of villains stand by. Mantis stands to the bottom left of the photograph.

• **Super Powers Fan Club:** included a charter member certificate, a color sticker, newsletter, deluxe patch, color photo and DC Comics subscriptions at reduced rates. The cost was $3 during the first issue and was raised to $3.50 during the second.

• **Steppenwolf Action Figure and Darkseid Adventure Record:** available for five proof of purchase seals from any Kenner **Super Powers** toy. The **Steppenwolf** figure came in a polybag and on the back of the record sleeve was a rebate coupon worth up to $3 on **Super Powers** toys. Collector **Jim Carlo** describes the 33-1/3" vinyl record: "It tells the story of the villainous **Darkseid** and his quest to rule the universe. It features **Batman** and **Robin** being attacked and captured by **Parademons**, with **Darkseid** sentencing them to **Desaad's** torture chamber. **Superman** saves the day by rescuing his fellow heroes of justice while, in the process, teeing off against both **Steppenwolf** and **Kalibak** in **Darkseid's** Arena of Doom. When all else fails, what's a villain like **Darkseid** to do? Why of course, the old 'Omega Effect' eyes trick! Who wins? Who loses? You decide!"

• **Child-sized Superman Cape:** offered for $1.50 plus three Kenner **Super Powers** proof of purchase seals.

• **Clark Kent Action Figure:** probably the most popular mail-in offer, he arrived by mail in a cardboard box for the cost of five Kenner **Super Powers** proof-of-purchase seals.

LISTINGS

SUPER POWERS COLLECTIONS (DC) (KENNER): 1985; 5" tall; fully dimensional; traditional colors; each could perform any number of actions, from punching to kicking.

FIRST SERIES: Subtract 25 percent for those found in Canadian blister packs, as these are more frequent and in less demand.

SUPERMAN: 1984; swinging fists; removable cape. Serial No. unknown.   **5**   **10**

BATMAN: 1984; swinging fists; removable cape. Serial No. unknown.   **10**   **20**

The Darkseid throne, shown here as the middle section of the Triceptor vehicle, fits into the back of the Destroyer's cockpit and can be lit by a button-triggered light. The light is between Darkseid's legs (in a brown box). The beam travels inside the chair and into the head of the throne via a fiber optic stem. When Darkseid is seated, the light enters the red plastic on the top of his head, making his "Omega eyebeams" light up. This throne also contains the battery pack (two D-cells) and can act as a lone vehicle. Flanking Darkseid are Brainiac (left) and Mantis (right). S. Kimball Collection.

The Tower of Darkness has Superman in its grips as Darkseid looks on. This photograph is from the Super Powers mini-catalogue which came with most accessories. S. Kimball Collection.

AQUAMAN: 1984; kicking legs; bronze trident. Serial No. 99650. **15 30**

ROBIN: 1984; right arm karate chops; removable cape. Serial No. unknown. **5 10**

WONDER WOMAN: 1984; arms swing up, deflecting with both wrists; golden lasso. Serial No. unknown. **5 10**

FLASH: 1984; legs move at "super" speed. Serial No. 99660. **7 14**

GREEN LANTERN: 1984; right swinging fist; plastic green lantern. Serial No. unknown. **15 30**

HAWKMAN: 1984; wings flap; mace. Serial No. unknown. **7 14**

JOKER: 1984; drops mallet; mallet; tails removable. Serial No. unknown. **7 14**

LEX LUTHOR: 1984; swinging fists; removable shoulder armor. Serial No. unknown. **10 20**

BRAINIAC: 1984; leg kicks; all chromed-plastic. Serial No. unknown. **5 10**

PENGUIN: 1984; umbrella lifts and drops; umbrella; tails removable. Serial No. 99690. **10 20**

SECOND SERIES: Had the same heroes and villians as the first series but added:

MARTIAN MANHUNTER: 1985; swinging fists; removable cape. Serial No. unknown. **7 14**

RED TORNADO: 1985; legs spin; removable cape. Serial No. unknown. **7 14**

FIRESTORM: 1985; swinging fists; removable cape. Serial No. unknown. **7 14**

GREEN ARROW: 1985; draws bow; two arrows and bow. Serial No. 99220. **10 20**

The Joker's mallet can also be used as a mask.

Detail on the back of Superman's cape.

DR. FATE: 1985; swinging fists; removable cape. Serial No. unknown.   **7   14**

KALIBAK: 1985; swinging fist; atom smasher weapon. Serial No. unknown.   **5   10**

MANTIS: 1985; swinging pincers. Serial No. unknown.   **7   14**

PARADEMON: 1985; flapping wings; yellow gun. Serial No. unknown.   **5   10**

DARKSEID: 1985; swinging fists; removable cape; eyes light up red when head section was lit. Serial No. unknown.   **2   5**

STEPPENWOLF: 1984; free with Darkseid record and $3 worth of coupons when you mailed in five proof of purchase seals from other **Super Powers** figures. Serial No. unknown.   **15   30**

STEPPENWOLF: 1985; raises axe; axe and backpack axe-holder. Serial No. 99970.   **7   14**

THIRD SERIES: Late 1985; had the same heroes and villians as the first and second series, but added:

CAPTAIN MARVEL (SHAZAM!): 1985; swinging fists; removable cape; Serial No. unknown.   **10   20**

MISTER MIRACLE: 1985; arms wave; removable cape; handcuffs. Serial No. 67180.   **7   14**

PLASTICMAN: 1985; neck pops up. Serial No. 67170.   **10   20**

The Green Lantern with his power lantern. Note the intricate ring on the right hand.

This series of photos show Lex Luthor with and without his armored "ultra suit."

A close-up of Hawkman's wing and mace. Note how the wings fit into the back of the figure.

Green Arrow's back is turned so that we may see a close-up of his quiver, bow, and arrows.

The first three photographs illustrate the different arm attachments for Cyborg.

MR. FREEZE: 1985; guns move on chest; arms move; removable helmet. Serial No. 67200.   **10   20**

CLARK KENT: 1985; free with five figures; mail to Kenner; expired May 31, 1986. Also could be ordered from Sears Wish book of 1985 with **Superman.** Serial No. unknown.   **25   50**

VEHICLES AND ACCESSORIES

NOTE: *All boxes had the **Super Powers** Collection logo, a field of blue with two parallel red stripes running up diagonally from left to right, inside the red stripes were a line of solid yellow stars. All boxes were marked as conforming with PS 72-76 safety standards. All boxes also displayed a small notice which explained that the pictures on the package might differ from the model enclosed.*

BATCOPTER: 1985; as described earlier.

Box size: 13-1/2" x 5" x 4-1/2". Box front showed illustration of **Batman** in Batcopter flying through Gotham City. Front of box lettered: "BATCOPTER", **"BATMAN'S AIR-PURSUIT CHOPPER"**; also three white star-balloons described basic functions. No photographs on end panels, just lettering. One side of box had photo of Batcopter front with **Batman** inside. Other side had photo of a side view of the Batcopter with its canopy up and **Batman** standing in front. The back had a series of four photographs:

(A) Small close-up of **Batman** in the Batcopter with the canopy open. Accompanying white box lettered: "THE CANOPY IS A PROTECTIVE SHIELD FOR **BATMAN**".

(B) Hand pushing nose cone release while nose cone ejects from front of Batcopter. White box lettered: "THE BLAST-OFF NOSE CONE KNOCKS DOWN VILLAINS. PULL UP FIGURES WITH THE WINCH".

GOLDEN PHAROAH: 1985; raises arms; staff. Serial No. 67230.   **7   14**

CYBORG: 1985; chrome/black flesh mix, three interchangeable chromed-plastic arms: drill, fist, and pliers. Serial No. 67150.   **15   30**

CYCLOTRON: 1985; torso twists, face plate. Serial No. 67160.   **7   14**

ORION: 1985; face spins from good to evil. Serial No. 67130.   **7   14**

SAMARI: 1985; raises fists; lightning sword. Serial No. 67220.   **7   14**

DESAAD: 1985; raises arms; shockers. Serial No. 99890.   **10   20**

TYR: 1985; shoots yellow missile/arm. Serial No. 67190.   **10   20**

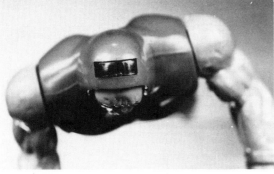

Here we see the top of the Darkseid figure's head. This wide band of transluscent red plastic connects the eyes. When the wide band is struck by light, the light travels to the eyes in a process similar to the way in which optic fiber light transfers.

This photo shows Cyclotron both with and without his face mask.

The two faces of Orion!

blades whirl. White box lettered: "CHOPPER BLADES SPINNING, **BATMAN** IS OFF TO FIGHT EVIL".
Serial No. 62270.   **35   70**

BATMOBILE: As described earlier.

There were two types of Batmobile boxes, though both were similar to other boxes in the **Super Powers** series. Each had several photos of **Batman** and **Robin** against a blue and yellow background. One of the two types of boxes had stars and white balloons with descriptive remarks similar to those on the Batcopter box; the other did not. Serial No. unknown.   **25   50**

SUPERMOBILE: 1984; as described earlier.

Box size: 9-1/4" x 7-3/4" x 3-3/4". Box front showed illustration of **Superman** in Supermobile flying through space, Lex-Soar 7 was chasing, firing lasers. Front of box lettered: "SUPERMOBILE", "SHIELDS **SUPERMAN** FROM KRYPTONITE!"; also had two white star-balloons describ-

(C) Hand holding Batcopter with nose almost straight up. **Penguin** hung from villain holder. White box lettered: "LOCK VILLAINS IN THE GRABBER — TURN THE BLADES AND WATCH THEM WHIRL".

(D) Hand holding back of Batcopter with bottom showing, other hand was twisting villain holder while rotor

On the planet of Apokolips, Mr. Miracle, Orion, and Cyclotron confront the "armed" Tyr. Tyr's rocket-arm is seen igniting from his shoulder. The evil Desaad peers from his hiding place off to the left. The only villain missing from these photographs is Mantis who is pictured in the Darkseid Destroyer photograph. S. Kimball Collection.

Here we see the extended ram of the Batmobile and the bottom of the Batmobile.

ing basic actions of vehicle. Perpendicular sides show Supermobile with canopy open, **Superman**, and **Aquaman**. Open side had **Aquaman** standing in front of Supermobile with **Superman** behind the vehicle. Closed side had **Superman** and **Aquaman** standing next to each other in front of Supermobile.

Back of box had three photos:

(A) Close-up of **Superman** in cockpit of Supermobile with canopy open. Accompanying white box lettered: "**SUPERMAN** JUMPS INTO THE CANOPY-COVERED COCKPIT TO BATTLE **LEX LUTHOR**".

(B) Hand holding Supermobile with battering ram extended toward a downed Lex-Soar 7. White box lettered: "THE SUPERMOBILE SHIELDS **SUPERMAN** FROM KRYPTONITE AS HE BATTLES THE EVIL **LEX LUTHOR** WITH THE KRYPTO-RAM!".

(C) Hand holding Supermobile from behind, **Braniac** was in villain holder. White box lettered: "**SUPERMAN** FLIES OFF TO THE HALL OF JUSTICE WITH THE VILLAINS SECURELY LOCKED IN THE CAPTIVATORS!".

Serial No.99760.   **20**   **40**

DELTA PROBE ONE VEHICLE: 1985; as described earlier.

Box size: 9-3/4" x 7-3/4" x 6-1/2". Box front showed illustration of **Robin** inside the Delta Probe One flying through space. Front of box lettered: "DELTA PROBE ONE", "BATTLING SPACESHIP OF THE **SUPER POWERS** HEROES"; also had three white star-balloons describing basic actions of vehicle. Perpendicular sides showed **Robin** at the front of the Delta Probe One.

Box back had four photos:

(A) Hand twisting cockpit activator and other hand on port back fin. Accompanying white box lettered: "**ROBIN** POSITIONS HIMSELF IN THE ROTATING COCKPIT AND ACTIVATES THE VILLAIN DETECTION-RADAR SYSTEM!"

(B) Hand pulling down the blue guns, opening the cockpit. White box lettered: "THE DELTA PROBE ONE GOES INTO ACTION AS **ROBIN** LOCATES THE VILLAIN, OPENS HIS PROTECTIVE CANOPY AND ENERGIZES THE STUN RAYS".

(C) Hand holding starboard back fin, back of Delta Probe One facing, **Lex Luthor** in villain catcher. White box lettered: "**ROBIN** TAKES OFF WITH **LEX LUTHOR** SAFELY TRAPPED IN THE VILLAIN CATCHER!"

(D) Hand on button under villain catcher, releasing blue bomb. White box lettered: "**ROBIN** DROPS THE DEMOBILIZER BOMB ON THE EVIL **LEX LUTHOR!**"

Serial No. 99850.   **20**   **40**

JUSTICE JOGGER: 1985; as described earlier.

Box size: 4-3/4" x 6-1/4" x 4-1/4". Box front showed illustration of **Superman** in Justice Jogger in rough terrain. Front of box lettered: "JUSTICE JOGGER", "OVERLAND VILLAIN CHASER"; also had one white star-balloon describing basic action of vehicle. Top of box had photo of **Superman** in Justice Jogger with the canopy down. Bottom of box had only lettering. Sides of box had **Superman** in Justice Jogger with the canopy down; **Wonder Woman** stood near.

Back had two photos:

(A) Close-up of **Superman** in Justice Jogger with the canopy up, the control panel in the down position. Accompanying white box lettered: "FLIP UP THE STEP — IT BECOMES A CONTROL PANEL — AND SWING DOWN THE PROTECTIVE SHIELD".

(B) Hand winding key on the side of the Justice Jogger with **Superman** inside. White box lettered: "TURN THE WINDUP RADAR DISH AND THE JUSTICE JOGGER TAKES OFF, GOING AFTER **DARKSEID** AND HIS CREW".

Serial No. 67280.   **10**   **20**

SUPER POWERS VEHICLE: 1985; as described earlier. Box detail and Serial No. unknown.   **NRS**

ALL TERRAIN TRAPPER: 1985; as described earlier. Box detail and Serial No. unknown.   **NRS**

HALL OF JUSTICE PLAYSET: 1984; as described earlier.

Box size: 25-1/2" x 17-1/2" x 7-3/4". Box front showed illustration of Hall of Justice to scale of the characters **Wonder Woman**, **Superman**, **Batman**, and **Robin** who stand in foreground. Supermobile and Batmobile are illustrated in background. Box lettered: "HALL OF JUSTICE", "HEADQUARTERS FOR THE BATTLE OF GOOD VS. EVIL"; also had five white star-balloons describing basic accessories of playset. One side panel had no illustrations, but lettering. Other side had three photos which usually appeared on the back of packages:

(A) Folded-up Hall of Justice. No white box, but caption under photo lettered: "PLAYSET IS COMPLETELY PORTABLE. OPEN IT UP TO CREATE ACTION-PACKED ADVENTURES!"

(B) Open Hall of Justice with child and various figures. Caption lettered: "**SUPERMAN** LANDS JUST IN TIME TO STOP A JAIL BREAK!"

(C) Close-up of Hall of Justice with figures. Caption lettered: "**LEX LUTHOR** BURSTS THROUGH THE SECURITY DOORS INTO THE COMPUTER COMMAND CENTER!"

Back of box had uncolored large illustration of photo (C) above and small illustration of photo (A) in upper right corner.

Serial No. 99830.   **50**   **100**

SET THE STAGE
FOR EXCITEMENT
WITH THESE ACTION FEATURES:

★ VEHICLE PAD FOR TAKE-OFF AND LANDING

2★ ELEVATOR PROVIDES QUICK ACCESS TO ROOF

3★ COMPUTER COMMAND CENTER TO
DIRECT OPERATIONS

★ WORKING SECURITY DOORS PROTECT
AGAINST ATTACK

5★ SECRET TRAP DOOR AND JAIL CELLS TO
CAPTURE VILLAINS

6★ SPECIAL CHAMBERS STORE AND
REVITALIZE UP TO 10 ACTION FIGURES

This listing appears on the back of the Hall of Justice box. S. Kimball Collection.

LEX-SOAR 7: 1984; as described earlier.

Box size: 9" x 7-1/2" x 3-1/2". Box front shows illustration of **Lex Luthor** in Lex-Soar 7 with **Superman** in the Supermobile close behind. Box lettered: "LEX-SOAR 7", "**LEX LUTHOR** ASSAULT SHIP!" Also had three white star-balloons describing basic actions of vehicle. Perpendicular sides have Lex-Soar 7, **Lex Luthor** and **Brainiac**. Open end side of box had **Lex Luthor** in front of the Lex-Soar 7 with **Brainiac** at the rear. Closed side had **Lex Luthor** in front of Lex-Soar 7 with **Brainiac** standing next to him.

Back side had three photos:

(A) Close-up of cockpit with canopy open and cables stretched from inside cockpit to armor on **Lex Luthor**. Accompanying white box lettered: "**LEX LUTHOR** LEAPS INTO THE CANOPY-COVERED COCKPIT TO BATTLE **SUPERMAN** THE POWER CABLES PLUG ONTO **LEX LUTHOR** ULTRA SUIT AND GENERATE ADDITIONAL POWER!"

(B) **Superman** in grappler. White box lettered: "LEX 'SEIZES THE ENEMY' WITH THE 'GRAPPLER CLAW'!"

(C) **Superman** on his knees below the Lex-Soar 7 with Kryptonite in the grappler. White box lettered: "LEX **LUTHOR** USES **KRYPTONITE** TO WEAKEN **SUPERMAN**!"

Serial No. 99730.   **20   40**

DARKSEID DESTROYER: 1985; as described earlier.

Box size: 19-3/4" x 11-3/4" x 10-3/4". Box front showed illustration of **Darkseid** in the Darkseid Destroyer flanked by **Kalibak** and **Desaad**; Delta Probe One was in the background. Box lettered: "DARKSEID DESTROYER", "FLYING FLAGSHIP OF THE ULTIMATE EVIL". Also five white star-balloons described basic actions of vehicle. Open ends of box were illustrated (uncolored) with the same design as front. One side had lettering but no illustration. Other side had five photographs that usually appeared on back of packages:

(A) and (B) Similar photos above each other of **Kalibak** and **Desaad** in their respective pods, strapped in. Accompanying white box was shared by both photos and lettered: "**KALIBAK** AND **DESAAD** MAN THE BATTLE STATIONS".

(C) **Darkseid** (with eyes lit up) pulling out from back of cockpit on throne. White box lettered: "**DARKSEID** PILOTS THE FLIGHT FROM HIS REMOVABLE COMMAND POST".

(D) Child pulling **Kalibak** on pod from main vehicle. White box lettered: "**DARKSEID'S** HENCHMEN DETACH FROM THE MAIN VEHICLE..."

(E) Shows Triceptor. White box lettered: "... AND JOIN THEIR LEADER TO FORM THE TRICEPTOR VEHICLE".

Back was uncolored, illustrated identically to front side of box. Serial No. 99830.   **50   100**

KALIBAK BOULDER BOMBER: 1985; as described earlier.

Box size: 9-3/4" x 8-3/4" x 6-1/4". Box front showed illustration of **Kalibak** in Boulder Bomber laying waste to city. Box lettered: "KALIBAK BOULDER BOMBER", "THE CRUEL CRUSHER'S MASSIVE MACHINE". Also four white star-balloons described basic actions of vehicle. Perpendicular sides have photos of **Kalibak** with Boulder Bomber. Open end had **Kalibak** in rear; closed end had **Kalibak** in front.

Back had four photographs:

(A) Boulder Bomber with mace launchers at different angles. Accompanying white box lettered: "THE SAVAGE **KALIBAK** CAREFULLY POSITIONS HIS DEADLY MACES AND LAUNCHES THEM AGAINST THE **SUPER POWERS** HEROES!"

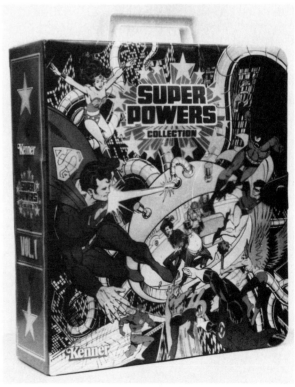

The Super Powers Collection Volume 1 carrying case had room for twelve figures and many small accessories. S. Kimball Collection.

(B) Shows one mace launching. This photograph shares the same white box as (A).

(C) Shows boulder being launched. White box lettered: "THE **KALIBAK BOULDER BOMBER** REALLY SHOWS ITS BRUTE FORCE AS THE AWESOME WARRIOR CATAPULTS THE BOULDER TO FELL HIS ENEMIES!"

(D) Shows close-up of front of Boulder Bomber. White box lettered: "NO ONE GETS IN THE WAY OF **KALIBAK** AS THE TEETH OF THIS VICIOUS VEHICLE GRIND INTO ACTION!" Serial No. 67020.   **25   50**

TOWER OF DARKNESS: As described earlier. Box detail and Serial No. unknown.   **NRS**

COLLECTOR'S CASE (Volume 1): 10" x 11" x 3-1/2" vinyl-covered case with yellow handle; closed on the sides with vinyl snaps. The case had various cubby holes for figures and small accessories, holding up to ten figures. A sheet of stickers, which could be applied to the cubby holes, was also provided.

The front of the case showed (clockwise) **Batman, Robin, Hawkman, Green Lantern, Aquaman, Flash, Superman,** and **Wonder Woman** surrounding the **Penguin, Joker, Braniac,** and **Lex Luthor.** The rear displayed blue stars surrounding a large yellow star, and the heroes from the front standing together to form a large inverted triangle. The spine had two yellow stars, the **Super Powers** logo, and the words "Kenner" and "Vol. 1".

On the inside of the front cover were four five-panel comic strips featuring (top to bottom) **Superman, Flash, Green Lantern,** and **Hawkman.** In the center were the words, "Secret Origins," in red letters. The inside rear cover also had four five-panel comic strips, these featuring **Batman, Robin, Wonder Woman,** and **Aquaman.** And, again, in the center are the words, "Secret Origins," in red letters.   **5   10**

The Clark Kent Action Figure given away by Kenner and sold by Sears. D. Fuchs Collection.

MAIL-IN OFFERS

FREE COLOR POSTER: as described earlier. Box unknown. Serial No. unknown.   **25   50**

SUPER POWERS FAN CLUB: as described earlier. Box unknown. Serial No. unknown.   **25   50**

DARKSEID RECORD: as described earlier. Box unknown. Serial No. unknown.   **25   50**

CHILD-SIZED SUPERMAN CAPE: as described earlier. Box unknown. Serial No. unknown.   **NRS**

CLARK KENT ACTION FIGURE: as described earlier; it was also available from Sears with a **Superman** figure in the 1985 Sears Wish book. Box unknown. Serial No. unknown.   **10   25**

These are the cups and boxes that were included in the Burger King Super Powers advertising campaign. At a cost of $.59 and during various weeks, you could purchase (left to right) Darkseid, Superman, Wonder Woman, and Batman. S. Kimball Collection.

All of these items carry the Super Powers logo. Each item is listed below and has a corresponding number in the illustration at right. S. Kimball Collection and illustration.

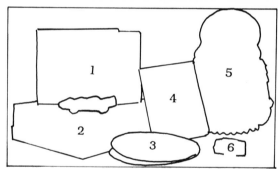

MORE SUPER POWERS COLLECTIBLES

DC Comics knew how to keep a good thing going. Besides creating an enormous selection of **Super Powers** figures and accessories, DC Comics licensed all kinds of products from pajamas to coloring books. Products carrying the **Super Powers** logo are easier to find than those with the **Secret Wars** logo. Most of the **Super Powers** products carried characterizations of **Batman**, **Robin**, and **Wonder Woman**. Occasionally, there were characterizations of the **Joker**, **Penguin**, **Lex Luthor**, and **Brainiac**, and less frequently, **Hawkman** and the **Flash**.

The marketing value of the **Super Powers** name is so great that DC Comics is still licensing products under this logo. Burger King, for example, ran a nationwide campaign, in early 1988, featuring **Super Powers** characters. The campaign was divided into two parts. The first part included four cups with **Batman**, **Darkseid**, **Superman**, and **Wonder Woman**, each on a yellow stand and detachable. The figures were similar to Kenner figures, but were not articulated. The second part featured a "Fun-Meal" box. With an order of a hamburger, french fries, and a soda, you received one of four different items ranging from a toothbrush holder to a figure.

The following is a partial listing of products licensed by DC Comics for the **Super Powers** Collection.

LISTINGS

(1) SUPER POWERS PLAY-DOH SET: 1985; set included molds to make **Batman**, **Robin**, **Superman**, **Wonder Woman**, **Joker**, **Penguin**, **Lex Luthor**, and **Brainiac**. Also included plastic play mat, Batmobile, and three cans of play-doh.   **15   30**

(2) SUPER POWERS SKYSCRAPER GAME: Parker Brothers, 1986; large blue box contained game. Object of game was to knock all of the villains off of the roofs!
10   20

(3) SUPER POWERS BIRTHDAY PARTY PLATES: 1986; blue paper plates with **Super Powers** logo and illustrated figures of **Super Friends**. Price per dozen.
2   5

(4) SUPER POWERS SIGNATURE STAMP SET: Fun-dimensions, 1985; stamp set included two stamping heads, paper, and ink. **5   10**

(5) SUPER POWERS BIRTHDAY PARTY CENTER-PIECE: 1986; colorful crepe and cardboard centerpiece with figures and logo as party plates. **2   5**

(6) SUPER POWERS FLASHLIGHTS: 1985; blue flashlight with **Super Powers** logo and **Batman. 5   10**

SUPER POWERS RING: Kenner, 1985; givaway white ring with red **Super Powers** logo. **.50   2**

BURGER KING/SUPER POWERS CUPS: 1987-88; each white cup had a different holder for various **Super Heroes**. Set included: **Darkseid**, **Superman**, **Wonder Woman**, and **Batman**.

Set:	20	40
Each:	5	10

The Kenner giveaway Super Powers Ring. S. Kimball Collection.

The collection of Remco's rendition of Archie Comics' Mighty Crusaders. S. Kimball Collection.

THE MIGHTY CRUSADERS

INTRODUCTION

The **Mighty Crusaders**, **The Fly**, **The Shield**, and the **The Web** of Archie (Red Circle) Comics Publications included some of "The World's Mightiest Heroes!" They were very realistic heroes, and, in retrospect, somewhat reminiscent of the heroes of DC Comics' **Watchmen** series. Though not always published by Archie Comics, the **Mighty Crusaders** have been around for ages. Unfortunately, they have been unknown to the general public.

MIGHTY CRUSADER FIGURES

The toys were not as impressive as the comic book. Although Remco Toys, Inc. was a noted toy manufacturer, especially during the 1960s and early 1970s, these five-inch action figures were considered the bottom of the line. Made of the same plastic as the figures in the Marvel **Secret Wars** collection, they were painted hastily and molded from dies with minimal detail.

The **Mighty Crusaders** figures were articulated at the head, shoulders, and hips, as were the Marvel **Secret Wars** figures. They were sold at the same time as the Marvel **Secret Wars** figures and were advertised as "Featuring Mighty Punch Action!" To activate the punch, the right arm was pulled back and released so that it sprung quickly forward.

The **Mighty Crusaders** figures were the first of their kind, in one respect; they were based on a series of characters that had never been merchandised before. Interestingly, of all the characters appearing in the **Mighty Crusaders** comic books, **The Fly** and **Fly Girl** were probably the most popular, yet these figures were not made.

OFFICIAL SECRET SONIC SIGNALING SHIELDS

The Official Secret Sonic Signaling Shields were basic shallow-hole whistles located at the top of a gray plastic-with-colored-decal shield. They came in a variety of designs, each reflecting its hero or villain. As in the Marvel **Secret Wars**, the problem was that only one figure of the action figure series actually carried a shield in the comic versions; in this case **The Shield**. The one-piece adjustable clip on the back of the shield allowed it to double as a ring.

WEAPONS

Besides the shield, each hero was equipped with at least one weapon, and, in most cases, a holster with a belt.

There were three types of weapons: a regular pistol always came with an accompanying holster, an

Shown are the eight plastic Official Secret Sonic Signaling Shields for the Mighty Crusaders. Above, from left to right, are shields which belonged to The Shield, The Comet, The Web, and The Fox. Below, left to right, are those which were carried by The Buzzard, The Brain Emperor, The Eraser, and the Sting. S. Kimball Collection.

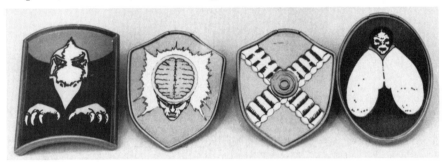

automatic machine gun with a shoulder sling, and a small machine gun with a bent stock that resembled a handgun grip, with a holster. Each gun was black and fit tightly into the figure's hand.

BLISTER PACKS

The blister pack boards were all printed at once without indicating the name of the featured character. Instead, a sticker was attached to the board, stating the character's name and whether he was "The Good" or "The Evil."

The back of the board was basic white stock with blue and gray printing and illustrations of each

figure, the specific shield and weapon pertaining to the character, and a descriptive paragraph about the character in the form of "*Power Data.*" This revealed the character's other identity, or Real Name, his Secret Identity, and his secret powers. The print also gave 1984 copyright and trademark information.

LISTINGS

All characters were flesh-colored plastic with spray-painted details. The only decals were on the shields. These figures were articulated at the shoulders and hips, and twisted at head and torso. *Power Data* appeared on the back of all blister packs.

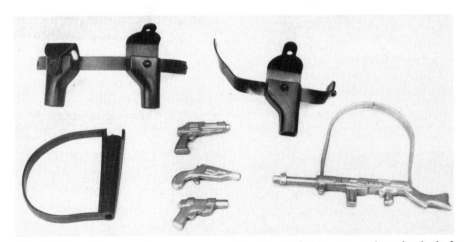

The different types of weapons used by the Mighty Crusaders included handguns and rifles, and their various holsters. S. Kimball Collection.

There were no large accessories or vehicles created for the **Mighty Crusaders**.

The World's Mightiest Heroes

THE SHIELD: Orange hair on blue Type 5 mask; red body with blue stripes on forearm; and red, white, and blue bodice. Accessories included holster/belt for two .45 caliber guns; rounded diamond-shaped shield with blue field of white stars and red and white stripes.

Power Data — Real Name, Joe Higgins; Secret Identity, FBI Agent. "**The Shield** has super-strength... and the power to leap great distances. His body could withstand 2,000 degrees of heat! His flame-proof costume also protects him from harm." **2**   **5**

THE FOX: Blue Type 4 mask with large fox ears on side, yellow eyes; blue body with yellow fox symbol on chest, yellow boots. Accessories included single holster/belt for one .45 caliber gun, also a rifle with sling; rounded diamond-shaped shield with blue field and yellow fox symbol.

Power Data — Real Name, Paul Patton; Secret Identity, Freelance Photographer. "Sworn enemy of all evil-doers. **The Fox** has turned his body into a living weapon, using karate and other martial arts along with his natural stealth and cunning." **2**   **5**

THE WEB: Green Type 5 mask; yellow and green bodice with green Type 4 web cape with Type 2 collar. Ac-cessories included holster/belt for two .45 caliber guns; oval-shaped shield with a green field of yellow web.

Power Data — Real Name: John Raymond; Secret Identity, Police Scientist. "**The Web** relies on his wits and fists to battle evil. Acting as a man of mystery to psychologi-cally inspire fear in criminals everywhere." **2**   **5**

THE COMET: Blue Type 5 mask with orange movable visor; blue torso with yellow stars and crescents, red arrow from waist to chest; red legs and feet. Accessories included sling/holster for sawed-off rifle; rounded diamond-shaped shield with field of blue with red and yellow comet and yel-low stars and crescents.

Power Data — Real Name, John Dickering; Secret Iden-tity, Scientist/Researcher. "He has the ability to burst into flame and fly like a living comet. He also has the ability to vaporize anything he gazes upon, forcing him to wear a protective visor." **2**   **5**

The Bad Guys

THE STING: Yellow skull face with one-half of a purple Type 4 mask on back of head; magenta and purple body with orange arms and legs; legs had small protrusions; and two fly-like magenta transparent wings on back, held on by yellow plastic. Accessories included one .45 caliber gun on holster/belt; oval-shaped shield with a field of purple with illustrated yellow wings with skull on top.

Power Data — Real Name, Unknown; Species, Un-known. "Victim of a DNA experiment gone bad, **The Sting**

The Buzzard was the only figure with a removable mask. S. Kimball Collection.

is half human, half insect. His retractable claws are capable of releasing a highly toxic venom for which there is no known cure." 2 5

THE ERASER: Green Type 5 mask; green and yellow body with yellow boots. Accessories included yellow crossing belt over shoulders with "Eraser" mechanism centered over chest; rifle with sling; rounded diamond-shaped shield with illustration of belt and eraser mechanism. Blister pack back illustration was incorrect, showing **Eraser's** shield as a rounded rectangle.

Power Data — Real Name, Unknown; Occupation, Professional Hitman and Super Assassin. "Using his energy-suit, **The Eraser** is capable of 'Erasing' objects making them vanish from this world sending them into an alternate limbo dimension." 2 5

THE BUZZARD: Orange removable "Pterodactyl"-type mask reveals flesh-toned bald head with green eyes and feathery white eyebrows; orange torso with purple and white gloves; blue legs with orange and white reptilian feet; red split cape. Accessories included sawed-off rifle; rounded rectangular shield with field of blue and red with illustrated yellow buzzard head and talons.

Power Data — Real Name, Malcolm P. Byrd; Occupation, Ex-Hunter and Sportsman. "**The Buzzard** is equipped with a specialized 'Flight Cloak' giving him mastery over the air. He is also armed with razor sharp talons." 2 5

THE BRAIN EMPEROR: Clear plastic cover on head revealed brain; orange body with yellow gloves and Type 4 cape with Type 2 collar; white skirt, flesh-toned legs, and blue boots. Accessories included sling-rifle; rounded rectangular shield with field of blue and **Brain Emperor's** face (top view) with glowing brain.

Power Data — Real Name, Unknown; Species, Mutant. "**The Brain Emperor's** mind grants him amazing psychic

The back of the blister packs gave information about each of the characters. S. Kimball Collection.

abilities such as: Telepathy, Hypnosis, Teleportation, Emphatic Projection and Psychokinesis." 2 5

Galoob's Defenders of the Earth figures are preparing to defend themselves against evil. From left to right: Flash Gordon and the Phantom, who is in the Phantom Copter, and Lothar stand ready for the attacks of Ming, riding Mongor, and his evil robot, Garax. Mandrake the Magician swoops down in the Defender's Claw Copter. Note the "Battle Action" knobs on the backs of the figures. S. Kimball Collection.

DEFENDERS OF THE EARTH
Men of Metal

The **Defenders of the Earth** action figures take you back to a day when toys were built to last. The six assorted figures were made of metal and coated with a plastic paint, and when compared with other figures of the day, the **Defenders of the Earth** were true heavyweights. On the average, they tipped the scales at one to four ounces more than the normal hollow plastic figures manufactured during the same period, and were 5-1/2" tall. Some of the figures were cloaked in what would now be considered elaborate capes. Both **Ming** and **Mandrake the Magician** had sturdy, two-ply, poly-fiber capes that

were sewn together with a long-lasting stitch. In contrast, **Super Powers** capes were a cut sheet of fabric connected to the figure by a tight-fitting plastic ring. All the **Defenders of the Earth** figures had small, black "Battle Action" knobs between their shoulder blades. When twisted, these knobs activated a swinging motion in the figures' arms.

Despite the fact that Lewis Galoob Toys, Inc., priced the excellent and elaborate **Defenders of the Earth** figures comparably to the **Super Powers** and **Secret Wars** figures, they did not sell nearly as well.

A close-up of Ming's collar as compared to that of Dr. Fate of the Super Powers Collection.

Some reason that the characters used were just too old for today's kids, though yesterday's kids would have recognized them easily.

Defenders of the Earth figures included three Super Heroes whose heyday had come and gone by the 1950s: **The Phantom**, **Flash Gordon**, and **Mandrake the Magician** were heroes of the comic strip world long before they entered comic books. **The Phantom**, however, still runs in new adventures each week in the newspapers and is one of the most popularly recognized characters, though, perhaps, not by the younger, toy-buying public. The hero figures were joined in their battle against evil by **Lothar**, **Mandrake's** long-time confidant and assistant. Together, the four were pitted against **Flash Gordon's** arch-nemesis, **Ming the Merciless**, and his ultimate evil robot, **Garax**, commander of the ice robot army.

The story of the modern **Defenders of the Earth** began in 1984 when the animated TV series began a weekday afternoon and early morning weekend run. It was very popular with the new generation of cartoon watchers, as well as the older "cartoonaholics" who recognized the virtual immortality of these Super Heroes. It is not known whether this popularity brought about the later creation of the toys, or if the toy concept came first, and the show was produced to advertise the figures. (This same uncertainty arose in the comic book world, with the advent of **Rom, Spaceknight** in the late 1970s. For more on this controversy, see the previous "From Toys to Comics" chapter.) In any case, it seems that the television program and the other usual media advertising could not satisfy Galoob Toys, and though no one at the toy or the comic companies will say who

came up with the idea, licensing the character toys to the comics, instead of the other way around, became a reality.

King Features, a major comic strip syndicate and owner of the rights to the **Defenders of the Earth** characters, licensed Marvel Comics to publish the **Defenders of the Earth** comic book. And this proved to be the correct choice. Marvel had a "child-directed" line, called Star Comics, that was aimed at 5 to 12 year olds. Star had already produced other toys-turned-comics such as **He-Man** and the **Masters of the Universe**, **Thundercats**, **Inhumanoids**, and **Silver Hawks**.

Defenders of the Earth issue No. 1 in January 1987 showed both the characters and their vehicles to be exactly like their toy counterparts. This issue described the origins of **The Phantom** and **Flash Gordon**, which was somewhat strange because **Lothar** and **Mandrake the Magician** were the two least known Super Heroes and, therefore, most

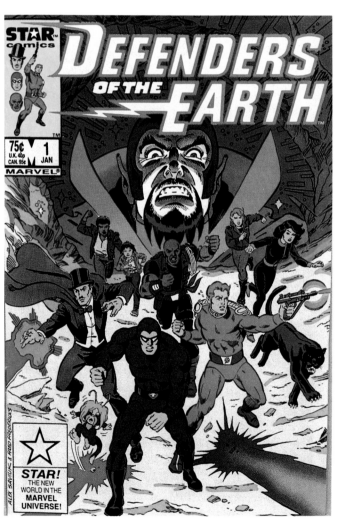

The first issue of Star's (Marvel Comics) Defenders of the Earth comic book. S. Kimball Collection. 1985/1988 Marvel Entertainment. All Rights Reserved.

Ming the Merciless gives his robot leader Garax final instructions before the take-off of Garax's Sword ship. S. Kimball Collection.

needed to have their origins told. But, perhaps, since the Star line was geared to an age group who did not know any of these 1950s heroes, all the origins needed telling. **Lothar** and **Mandrake's** origins were subsequently told in the next issue of the comic.

LISTINGS

FLASH GORDON: Blonde hair with flesh-toned face; red body with yellow epaulets and collar border; black belt with yellow and white embossings; red legs and black boots. Accessories included black sword and pistol.

3   7

GARAX: White icy features with two triangular red and black eyes, pentagonal mouth with vertical red and black stripes; icy-block body featured with a hexagonal portrait of **Ming** on the belly. Accessories included red freeze-ray arm unit and pistol.

7   15

LOTHAR: Bald brown flesh-toned, with black eyebrows; black body suit with green and white vest over top of torso, gold medallion on chest; white sash around waist and white and green embossing on legs; white boots with green details. Accessories included black grappling hook with cord and pistol.

7   15

MANDRAKE THE MAGICIAN: Black top hat on flesh-toned head, black hair and moustache; body made up of black tuxedo with red vest, white shirt, and black tie; black shoes and black and red cloth cloak. Accessories included long magic black wand.

10   20

MING THE MERCILESS: Purple covered cowl on green face with black eyebrows and beard, pointed green ears; purple body with bright red and yellow details on torso and trunks; green hands; brown boots and purple and red Type 4 cape. Accessories included long red serpent septer and red pistol.

3   7

THE PHANTOM: Purple covered cowl on flesh-toned face with black Type 1 mask; purple body unremarkable except for black belt with silver buckle (which was unlike the comic version in which he wore striped trunks); black boots. Accessories included black whip and pistol.

7   15

ACCESSORIES

DEFENDERS CLAW COPTER: White one-man helicopter with red interior and clear canopy; red and blue "D" decal on sides of fuselage; black landing claws and white aft support landing column; assorted red and blue bombs on fins; gray rotor with red and black decals.

15   30

FLASH SWORDSHIP: Blue fighter with four perpendicular wings and canopy centered over top; transparent canopy with red interior; black handle protruded from rear of vehicle; red and yellow decals throughout; red sword triggered from underneath, jutting out the sword blade.

10   20

GARAX SWORDSHIP: Purple fighter with four perpendicular wings and canopy centered over top; transparent canopy with purple interior; black handle protruded from rear of vehicle; black and pink decals throughout; silver and purple sword triggered from underneath, jutting out the sword blade.

10   20

GRIPJAW: White vehicle with red and black decals; standing operations panel on rear, blue jaws with white teeth and decals on front; as Gripjaw was pushed, the jaws opened and closed. **15 30**

MONGOR: Purple serpent with protruding spines on head and dragon face with red tongue; light purple details over long, purple body ending in an arrow point; purple saddle centered over break in body; wheels concealed at the base of the first and second hump. **10 20**

PHANTOM SKULL COPTER: Purple one-man helicopter with purple interior and skull-shaped red translucent canopy; black landing claws and gray aft support landing column; assorted purple and black bombs on fins; black rotor with purple and white decals. **15 30**

The Teenage Mutant Ninja Turtles (left to right) Donatello, Raphael, Leonardo, and Michaelangelo assemble to protect their master, Splinter (back left), from the evil Shredder (center). S. Kimball Collection.

PLAYTHINGS
TEENAGE MUTANT NINJA TURTLES
Heroes in a Half Shell

The following chapter is based on a press release from Playmates Toys, Inc., received from Diane Horton, Director of Marketing at Playmates Toys on February 29, 1988. We would like to thank Diane for her assistance with this chapter, which gives an exclusive look into the newest Super Hero action figures.

*In the 1930s **Superman**, **Buck Rogers**, and **Flash Gordon** personified the birth of Super Heroes; the Turtles show you the future!*

They've been lurking underground for years. Now they're hitting the streets — not to mention the TV screens of America — with a tongue-in-cheek vengeance.

Their motto: *"Strike hard and fade away ... into the night."*

Their arch-nemesis: The evil **Shredder**, master of ninjitsu, whose very name evokes the cool, cutting efficiency of a cheese grater.

Who are they? ...Heroes in a half shell!

The current rage of **Teenage Mutant Ninja Turtles** is a new dawn for Super Hero action figures. Animals have appeared before, such as the **Secret Wars' Fal-** con mascot, **Redwing**, and **Krypto the Superdog**, included with the **Superman** outfit of **Captain Action**; but never have animals been the lead characters in an action figure line.

The original comic book, co-created by New Englanders Kevin Eastman and Peter Laird, features the adventures of four teenage turtles. Altered in form and intelligence by a mysterious radioactive ooze, the **Turtles** spent 13 years training with **Splinter**, a wise old sewer rat, in the secret arts of the Ninja — the shadow warriors of feudal Japan.

Teenage Mutant Ninja Turtles are here and now. The press release package had "Fresh from the sewer" on the cover. This brilliant marketing strategy did not include heroes from other planets, detectives in capes, radioactive spiders, or special rays and drugs. As one of the press releases put it: **"Teenage Mutant Ninja Turtles** are the first alternative Super Heroes. Take ordinary hard-shell turtles, transform them with radioactive ooze into intelligent adolescent beings, and you get COMEDY-action adventure."

The four wisecracking martial artists are destined to be the off-the-wall hit of the toy industry for quite

The evil Shredder (left) stands next to Splinter (right), the rat mutation of a Ninja master who trained the Turtles to fight for their share of pizza. S. Kimball Collection.

This series of cartoon panels re-tells the origins of the Turtles and Splinter from page two of Plaything's advance catalogue. S. Kimball Collection.

Close-ups of the Teenage Mutant Ninja Turtles. Above, left to right are Leonardo, the commander, and Michaelangelo, the party reptile. Below, left to right, are Donatello, the brain, and Raphael, the wit. S. Kimball Collection.

a few years. Richard Sallis, Playmates Toys vice president of marketing, stated, "When the smoke clears, the industry will be shell-shocked."

According to statistics released with the press package, the average boy in the five to nine age group collects about $300 worth of action figures and accessories. In 1987, the male action figure and accessories category of the toy market pulled in $1 billion in retail sales.

Though the line made its debut in January, the **Turtles** did not hit the toy shelves until late May 1988. The first series feature six highly-detailed 4-1/2" action figures articulated at the neck, shoulders, forearms, and hips. They are backed by a $5 million TV advertising campaign to run throughout late 1988.

This promotion does not include the short TV series which ran between Christmas 1987 and January 1988. The four episodes excellently told the story of **TMN Turtles**, from their origin through their first adventure. It also included appearances by most of the accessories that are now being produced for the action figures.

The four leading Turtles are:

LEONARDO: Perfectionist and unofficial commander of the team, uses keen eyesight and acute hearing to spearhead the **Turtle** assaults; he is armed with Katana Blades.

MICHAELANGELO: Wild party reptile with pizza in one hand and trusty Nunchukus in the other.

DONATELLO: Creative genius and designer of the **Turtle** attack vehicles, and the brains behind the **Turtle's** brawn; he is armed with a pair of Bo.

RAPHAEL: Boasts a rapier wit, that keeps everyone in stitches; he is armed with a pair of forked Sai.

FIGURES

The **Turtles** are dressed in a black belt with various weapons, knee pads, arm pads, veins popping from their biceps, tied-on masks, and asssorted "grins" showing bared teeth. In addition to the **Turtles**, there are the two figures of **Splinter** and **April O'Neil**. Both are fully detailed and posable.

The evil side of this series includes the **Shredder** and his "Slice 'n Dice Armor," **Behop**, a pig-like mutant with a Shell Drill, **Rocksteady**, a rhino with a Retro Gun, and a **Foot Soldier** with a Shell Biter.

Each figure comes in a color blister pack. Most figures also have a Deluxe Weapons Assortment, and

Donatello in his blister pack with Deluxe Weapons Assortment. S. Kimball Collection.

The many workings of a Teenage Mutant Ninja Turtle figure. Courtesy of Playmates Toys.

From left to right are April, Foot Soldier, Rocksteady, and Behop. Courtesy of Playmates Toys.

"Join the Turtle Force Fan Club!!" This small sheet was included with each figure of the first series. S. Kimball Collection.

all come with a small Turtle Force Fan Club membership application.

ACCESSORIES

Riding the Turtle Party Wagon, our heroes roll into town in their shell-topped battle wagon. "Engage the spring-loaded 'Tenderizer' side weapon to soften the most callous Foot soldier. Drop wacko itchy powder and laughing gas bombs! Launch sneak attacks with the surprise front panel that drops down to release **Turtle** figures and bombs!" This party van features machine guns, control chairs, and more.

"The Turtle Blimp is an inflatable 30"-long blimp and comes with 'Turtlized' armor printing, flight fins, and loops for hanging from the ceiling!" Included are bomb launchers, an infrared scope, and vinyl patch kit. The Detachable Glider has rolling wheels for ground play, and the Turtle trigger launches all figures and wacko bombs into battle, individually or all together!

The Turtle Party Wagon is equipped to do battle as well as to provide the "Motor-vation" for our team of half-shell heroes. Courtesy of Playmates Toys.

The Turtle Trooper brings the Turtle Blimp to the ground. This accessory really works. The 22" parachute can be tossed into the air and the unique delay system opens the chute at maximum height, while its speed fins automatically convert to blasters. This low-end **Turtle** accessory also features an armored back pack, official **Turtle** pennant, **Turtle** control handles, and adjustable helmet and visor.

Cheapskate is the **Turtle's** radical street-legal skateboard. The spring-loaded **Turtle** leg kicks, and the sewer skater becomes pizza-powered, with a remote throttle control.

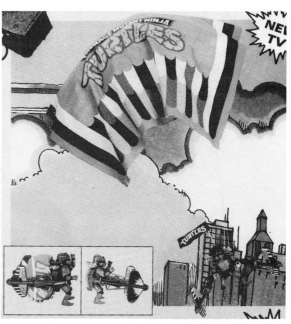

Floating gracefully to the ground, Raphael (with safety helmet on) is ready for action in the 22" Turtle Trooper. Courtesy Playmates Toys.

The bad guys have their share of accessories, too. The Technodrome is about 22" tall and 22" wide. The evil Foot Clan's powerhouse on wheels blasts with a rock blasting cannon; Eyeclops scouts out the **Turtles** blimp; blasters fire; these and many other details make this a facinating toy as well as a piece of art.

The Knucklehead is a "knuckle-sandwich" maker in a vehicle that resembles a spider. When dropped along a web, spring-loaded arms automatically grasp victims on contact, reel them in, and then punch them with boxing-gloved hands.

There are also three sets of Gags, Jokes & Crazy Weapons Assortments. Each set comes with pranks, jokes, and figure-sized accessories from pizzas and sewer covers to plungers and **Turtle** eggs.

The Turtle Battle Fun Assortment allows you to become a real mutant **Turtle** with kid-sized equipment.

Each set features "fun action" accessories, including an official **Turtle** weapon, color-matched elbow pads, knee pads, and Ninja mask with **Turtle** nose.

...And so the battle rages. They may not slay the **Shredder** *and they may not prevent galactic warfare on earth, but the* **Teenage Mutant Ninja Turtles** *will laugh trying.* (And so will any collector who purchases these items. These will be *hot* collectors' items in a very short time!)

LISTINGS

FIGURES

All figures are 4" to 4-1/2" tall, articulated at shoulders, hips, neck, and forearms. All prices are 1988 retail prices.

LEONARDO: Dark green turtle, mouth open showing teeth on right side of face; with blue headband, elbow, forearm, and knee pads; black sash with "L" in center with crossing bands over shoulders; includes two yellow Katana Blades.   --   **4**

MICHAELANGELO: Blue-green turtle, mouth open showing teeth on left side of face; with orange headband, elbow, forearm, and knee pads; black sash with "M" in center without crossing bands; includes yellow Nunchukus.   --   **4**

DONATELLO: Olive green turtle, mouth open showing teeth on both sides of face; with purple headband, elbow, forearm, and knee pads; black sash with "D" in center with two crossing bands on right shoulder; includes two Bo.   --   **4**

RAPHAEL: Light green turtle, mouth open showing teeth on both sides of face as well as center; red headband, elbow, forearm, and knee pads; black sash with "R" in center without crossing bands and Sai holders flanking center sash tie; includes two Sai.   --   **4**

SPLINTER: Brown rat with two incisors under black nose; red robe covers body with black sash; rat tail from

Donatello and his Deluxe Weapons Assortment. Note that a weapons rack is included. S. Kimball Collection.

behind; brown legs with gray bands on ankles; includes light brown Ninja bow with arrow.   --   **4**

APRIL O'NEIL: Brown-haired woman with yellow clothes rolled up at elbows; white belt and shoes; includes black .45 automatic and camcorder.   **TBA**

SHREDDER: Flesh-toned figure with blue helmet and magenta face mask; magenta cape extends to a point on the center of the chest; blue "Slice 'n Dice" elbow, shin, and tricep pads; black tights with black sash; magenta boots.   --   **4**

BEHOP: Light brown pig face with dual incisors at the tip of the snout and flanking underbite fangs extending from the lower lip, blue glasses, brown mohawk; bare arms with gray wristbands and turtle shell shoulder pads; bare chest with rust-colored vest and white necklace; black rolled-up pants with chain-link belt; brown shoes without socks; includes gray shell drill and bronze trash can lid.   **TBA**

ROCKSTEADY: Gray rhino head with two horns, red eyes and small teeth on either side of face, green turtle helmet with ears sticking out; bare arms with black wristbands; bare chest with black body shirt; black sash on camouflaged pants and World War I-style army boots, turtle shell thigh pads; includes retro gun rifle and gray sewer cover shield.   **TBA**

FOOT SOLDIER: Magenta elongated head with yellow "bug eyes" as feature, red mohawk stripe on head; gray arms with large blue pads extending from wrists, black wristbands; chest is shielded with part of head armor, gray tunic with black sash underneath; gray pants with black leggings; unremarkable magenta bare feet; includes shell biter weapon.   **TBA**

ACCESSORIES

All accessories include a Turtle jokebook.

TURTLE PARTY WAGON: Large butterscotch and olive-green van with orange guns mounted on side mirrors, orange radar dish atop turtle shell roof, butterscotch-colored spoiler on roof. All windows are cut out, without panes. Orange swivel chair swings out from inside the van and a step folds out of the door. Bumper on front drops down to release two bombs: one of Laugh Gas, the other of Itchy Powder. Van is large enough to hold six figures.   **TBA**

TURTLE BLIMP: Green vinyl 30" long blimp with many lithographed details.   Four green fins with embossed hydraulic hinges encircle rear of blimp. Underneath is detachable green glider with four wacko bombs including Sleep Dust, Itchy Powder, Laugh Gas, and Stink-O. Detachable glider has yellow wheels to roll on and a control chair on front with decaled controls, handlebars, and

The Turtle Blimp launches a few bombs, as well as Donatello, while gliding over a recent Shredder-produced battlefield. Courtesy of Playmates Toys.

The Cheapskate, seen in this publicity illustration, is still being produced. Illustration courtesy of Playmates Toys Inc. 1988 Mirage Studios. All Rights Reserved.

The Technodrome is being produced. Illustration courtesy of Playmates Toys Inc. Copyright 1988 Mirage Studios. All Rights Reserved.

red guns centered on the front of the chair. Green and orange turbo jets flank chair. Includes vinyl patch kit.

TBA

TURTLE TROOPER: 22" green cloth parachute with **"TEENAGE MUTANT NINJA"** in white letters on red field atop yellow and green **"TURTLES"** in center; red, white, and blue stripes on perimeter; speed fin has green decal with red, white, and blue stripes which, when activated, flips to blasters with red, orange, yellow, and white decal resembling explosion. Green helmet resembles medieval knight's helmet with adjustable visor. Red pennant has yellow **"TURTLES"** in center.

TBA

A Foot Soldier works the controls of the Knucklehead as it captures the commander of the Turtles, Leonardo. Courtesy of Playmates Toys.

CHEAPSKATE: Green skateboard with wide red trucks and fan on back. Yellow detachable flashlight in front. Chrome engine under fan with black wire throttle control and silver mufflers flanking board. Includes red pennant with yellow **"TURTLES"** in center and black sewer cover shield.

TBA

TECHNODROME: White 22" high x 22" wide sphere, heavily embossed and decaled. Blue bands on diameter with small blue sphere on top with white, red, and blue eyeball "Eyeclops" inside. Two large red cannons on forward and rear. Inside are compartments to hold 15 figures. Blue detachable Technorovers with two red "Eyespy" missiles and cannon. Includes armor patch kit.

TBA

KNUCKLEHEAD: Gray control chair with decaled controls on floor and inside front of chair, red foot on black decal on sides of control chair; two blue eyes with red dumbbell-shaped feelers on front of chair; four blue flanking legs underneath resembling a spider's. Back three legs on each side have purple boxing gloves attached to ends, forward two legs have grasping hands attached with purple shields on forearms. String attaches from underside through top of control chair.

TBA

GAGS, JOKES & CRAZY WEAPONS ASSORTMENTS

All assortments include figure-sized weapons.

SET #1: Includes green **Turtle** ring connected to squeeze bulb to squirt water "fresh from the sewer," joke

TURTLE BATTLE FUN ASSORTMENT™

Be a real mutant Turtle just like our green teen Turtle heroes! Kids will be shellshocked as Leonardo, Raphael and Michaelangelo come to life with this assortment of kid-sized accessories. Each set features fun action accessories, including official Turtle weapon, color matched elbow pads, knee pads, and Ninja mask with Turtle nose! 11 pieces in all. Ages 4 and up.

Stock #5026 Std. Pk.: 12 Carton Wt.: 7.5 lbs. Std Pk. Cube: 3.6

Leonardo
Pretend you're Leonardo, the battle commander of the Turtles! Set includes one Katana Blade sword, blue Ninja mask with Turtle nose, blue knee and elbow pads, belt and buckle with Turtle logo, mag flying disc, Leo's favorite jokes and label sheet with insignias and wacky Turtle phrases!

Raphael
Become Raphael, the witty voice of the Turtles! Set includes two sais, red Ninja mask with Turtle nose, red knee and elbow pads, belt and buckle, sewer cover flying disc, Raph's favorite jokes and label sheet.

Michaelangelo
Be a party reptile like Michaelangelo, the wild and crazy Turtle! Set includes nunchukus, orange Ninja mask with Turtle nose, orange elbow and knee pads, belt and buckle, pizza flying disc, Mike's favorite jokes and label sheet.

GAGS, JOKES & CRAZY WEAPONS ASSORTMENT

It'll be a laugh riot when you become a practical joker just like the wild and crazy Turtles! Fool family, friends and the Foot with this assortment of real pranks and hilarious Turtle jokes. And heat up the fun and action with the crazy figure-sized accessories included in each set! Ages 4 and up.

Stock #5030 Std. Pk.: 24 Carton Wt.: 6.8 lbs. Std Pk. Cube: 8

Set #1
Join the Turtle team with the official Turtle Ring that actually squirts "fresh from the sewer" water! Set includes squirt ring with Turtle logo, Turtle jokebook and four crazy figure-sized accessories - sewer cover shield, mag flyer, boom box radar, and sewerpipe bazooka!

Set #2
Write secret messages to the Turtles with Invisible Turtleshell Ink! The words magically appear when exposed to heat! And blast the Foot with the Retromutogen Squirter! Watch Shredder's reaction as the green liquid magically disappears in seconds. Set includes Invisible Turtleshell Ink powder, Retromutogen Squirter, jokebook, and four crazy figure-sized weapons - garbage can shield, pizza flyer, sewer slingshot, and city communicator.

Set #3
Communicate in the sewers like a real mutant Turtle! It's the "Turtle Call" razzer, the ultimate insult to the Foot Clan! And take a peek at Mutant Turtle Eggs, a devious Turtle package that gives the Foot a real jolt when opened. Great prank for family and friends! Set includes Mutant Turtle Eggs in envelope, Turtle Call, jokebook and four crazy figure-sized weapons - no Foots shield, rock 'n roll flyer, sewer stopper and sewer searchlight.

This page from the advance press package shows the Battle Fun Assortment and Gags, Jokes & Crazy Weapons Assortments. Illustration courtesy of Playmates Toys Inc. Copyright 1988 Mirage Studios. All Rights Reserved.

book #1. Weapons include sewer cover shield, mag-wheel cover flyer, boom box radar, and sewer pipe bazooka.

TBA

SET #2: Includes green and white tube of invisible ink powder, Retromutogen squirter, joke book #2. Weapons include garbage can shield, pizza flyer, sewer slingshot, and white city communicator. **TBA**

SET #3: Includes red and green Turtle Call razzer, Mutant Turtle eggs in envelope, joke book #3. Weapons include No Foots Shield, record-shaped rock 'n roll flyer disc, plunger-type sewer stopper, and box-shaped sewer searchlight. **TBA**

TURTLE BATTLE FUN ASSORTMENTS

All assortments are child-sized accessories which include green **Turtle** nose and joke book with label sheet.

LEONARDO SET: Includes one blue Katana Blade sword with gray blade, blue Ninja mask; blue elbow and knee pads, belt and buckle, and Mag flying disc. **TBA**

RAPHAEL SET: Includes two red sais with gray blades, red Ninja mask, red elbow and knee pads, belt and buckle, and sewer cover flying disc. **TBA**

MICHAELANGELO SET: Includes orange nunchukus with gray chain, orange Ninja mask, orange elbow and knee pads, belt and buckle, and pizza flying disc. **TBA**

Appendix I
CHARACTER DESCRIPTIONS

The following descriptions correspond to the illustrations on the facing pages. The characters listed here are major comic book characters who have been made into more than one series of action figures. The descriptions are of the characters as they appeared in the comic books, not necessarily as they appeared as action figures. Please note the copyright on each character.

AQUALAD: No mask; black hair, full torso red chain mail armor with sleeves; red briefs with black belt and gold "A" buckle; no tights and black boots; black gloves. Copyright 1988 DC Comics.

AQUAMAN: No mask; blonde hair; full torso orange chain mail armor with sleeves; green briefs with black belt and gold "A" buckle; green tights and fins on boots; green gloves. Accessories included trident and sea horse. Copyright 1988 DC Comics.

BATGIRL: Long black hair on female flesh-toned face with blue Type 5 mask; gray bodysuit with gold Batsymbol; blue boots. Accessories included Batarang. Vehicle: Batgirl Cycle. Copyright 1988 DC Comics.

BATMAN: Type 3 dark blue mask without ears, tall, flat "bat" ears were vertical from either side of head; full torso and sleeves of gray fabric with yellow and black Batsymbol centered on chest; wide yellow Bat utility belt on dark blue briefs; gray tights and dark blue boots, boots have blue fins on back; dark blue gloves with blue fins on back. Accessories included Batarang. Vehicles: Batmobile (two types), Batcycle, Batcopter, Batplane, and Batboat. Copyright 1988 DC Comics.

BUCK ROGERS: There are various descriptions of Buck Rogers from a basic astronaut to a Roman gladiator to a 1980s TV show. Copyright owner is unknown.

CAPTAIN AMERICA: Type 3 blue mask with "A" centered on forehead and tiny white wings on either side of head; full torso and sleeves of blue chain mail with star centered on chest, red and white vertical stripes around torso; black belt on blue briefs; blue tights and red boots with cuffs; red gloves with cuffs. Accessories included red, white, and blue circular shield. Copyright 1988 Marvel Comics Group.

The Captain America Shield. Color scheme (from outside in) is red-white-red and then a circular field of blue with a centered white star. S. Kimball Illustration. TM Marvel Comics 1988.

CAPTAIN MARVEL (SHAZAM!): No mask, black hair; full torso and sleeves of red with yellow fabric lightning bolt centered on chest; Type 3 white cape with Type 1 collar with yellow trim; red tights with yellow Type 2C boots; forearms end in yellow bands, no gloves. Copyright 1988 DC Comics.

CATWOMAN: Long black hair on female head with purple Type 5 mask with cat ears over ears; purple body suit; black belt and boots. Copyright 1988 DC Comics.

The basic Batsymbol seen on most Batparaphenalia. S. Kimball Illustration. TM DC Comics 1988.

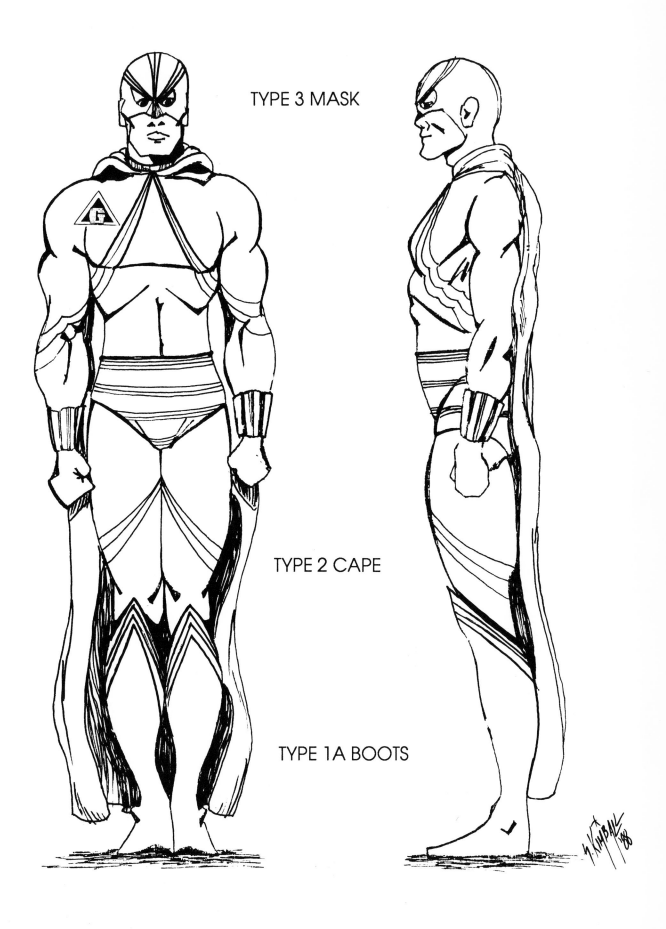

TYPE 3 MASK

TYPE 2 CAPE

TYPE 1A BOOTS

TYPE 1 MASK

TYPE 4 CAPE w/
TYPE 2 COLLAR

TYPE 2A BOOTS

DAREDEVIL: Type 3 red mask with small "horns" flanking forehead; full torso and sleeves of red cloth with diagonal "DD" on chest in black outline; red belt on red briefs; red tights with holster for night stick; red boots and gloves. Accessories included night stick with or without grappling hook. Copyright 1988 Marvel Comics.

The notorious "DD" symbol on Daredevil's chest. S. Kimball Illustration. TM Marvel Comics 1988.

DOCTOR DOOM: Type A (with robe), Type 4 metal mask with square slits for eyes, nose is folded out, mouth slit has crossbars, covered in monk-type robe; full torso and sleeves of metal, torso covered in green robe with two large, round gold clasps holding cape to shoulders; thin belt with centered "D"; detailed metal legs and boots; metal arms and gauntlets. Accessories included jet-backpack under robe and various guns. Copyright 1988 Marvel Comics.

DOCTOR DOOM: Type B (without robe), mask identical to Type A; torso covered in tight green fabric with "electronics" detail in black outline; wide black belt with buckle on tight green fabric briefs, legs, boots, and arms. Copyright 1988 Marvel Comics.

DOCTOR OCTOPUS: Type 1 mask (or large glasses), black hair; green upper torso from wide yellow belt to neck; two flanking sets of long, thin metallic arms with either flat round pads or two pincers at the end of the arm; green briefs and legs with yellow boots, green arms, and yellow gloves. Copyright 1988 Marvel Comics.

ELECTRO: Green Type 3 mask with large yellow lightning bolts pointing from face outward; green bodysuit, black belt, and green briefs; green legs with yellow boots; green arms with yellow gloves. Copyright 1988 Marvel Comics.

FALCON: White Type 5 mask with red detail on nose, brown flesh tone, black hair; white bodysuit with cut-away "V" from shoulders, black belt, and red briefs; red legs with white boots with yellow triangle on toe resembling talons; arms are bare from triceps to gloves. Accessories included red wings attached to back and extending behind arms and brown eagle sidekick. Copyright 1988 Marvel Comics.

FLASH: Red Type 3 mask with small yellow wings flanking sides of head; bodysuit was entirely red with "Flash" symbol centered over chest; lightning bolts encircled wrists and ankles; yellow boots had white wings on ankles. Copyright 1988 DC Comics.

FLASH GORDON: No mask, blonde hair, blue eyes; outfit usually red with gold epaulets and collar detail; navy blue pants with black boots and belt. Copyright 1988 King Features.

GREEN ARROW: Short blonde hair on male face with green Type 1 mask; flesh-toned with green and black outfit, black boots; accessories included quiver with arrows and bow. Copyright 1988 DC Comics.

GREEN HORNET: Green or black Type 2 mask, black or green fedora hat; green business suit with white shirt and green tie; black or brown shoes. Accessories included cane with hornet tip. Copyright unknown.

GREEN LANTERN: Green or black Type 2 mask, brown or black hair; green and white bodysuit with black legs; white boots and gloves. Accessories included green ring and green lantern. Copyright 1988 DC Comics.

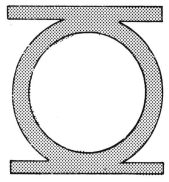

The symbol for the Green Lantern Corps. S. Kimball Illustration. TM DC Comics 1988.

HULK: Black hair on grimacing green face; green skin with torn magenta pants and rope belt (however, currently the Hulk appears with gray skin in the comic books). Copyright 1988 Marvel Comics.

HUMAN TORCH: No mask, features: red, orange, and yellow and resembled a burning face; body was similar with virtually no features, but with flames. Copyright 1988 Marvel Comics.

IRON MAN: Type 4 golden iron mask with simple slits for eyes and mouth, face mask was flanked by red armor that extended to other side of head, flat, round, ears on either side of head; red torso armor with yellow circle on chest and red circular pods on thighs; yellow legs and arms; red gauntlets and boots with cuffs. Copyright 1988 Marvel Comics.

JOKER: No mask, wild green hair, and white face with large red-lipped mouth; purple pin-striped jacket covering white shirt and green tie; purple pin-striped pants; white gloves and black wing tip shoes. Copyright 1988 DC Comics.

LIZARD: Reptilian features like namesake, complete with forked tongue; torso was covered in black turtleneck shirt with white lab coat; tattered pants were magenta with green lizard tail from rear end. Copyright 1988 Marvel Comics.

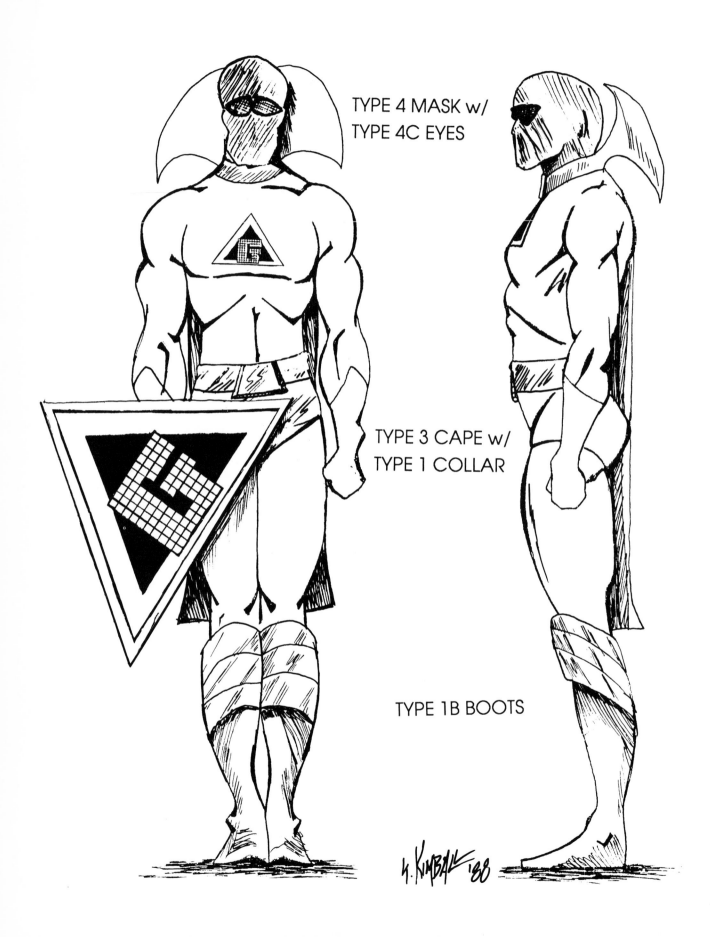

TYPE 4 MASK w/
TYPE 4C EYES

TYPE 3 CAPE w/
TYPE 1 COLLAR

TYPE 1B BOOTS

S. KIMBALL '88

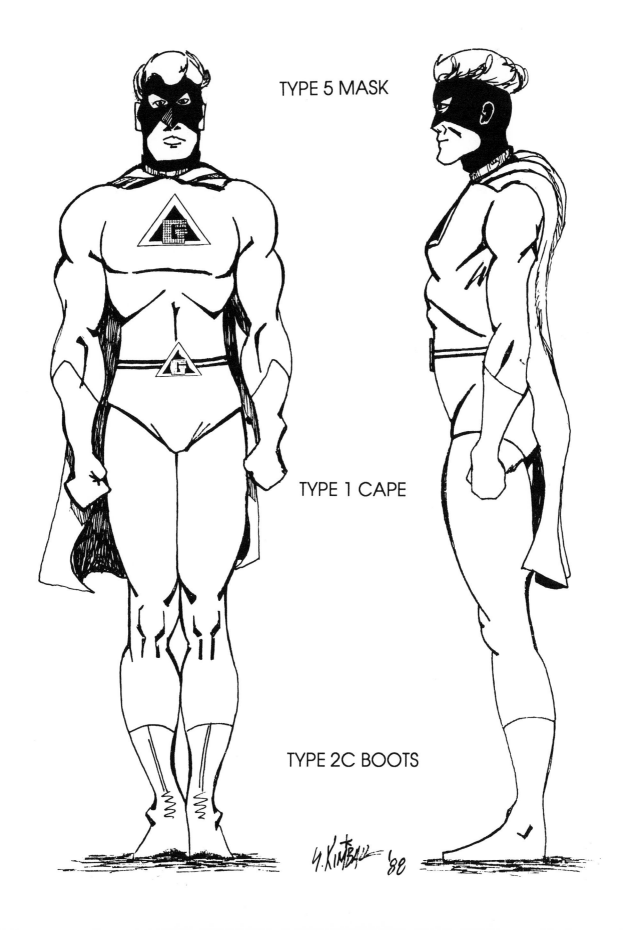

TYPE 5 MASK

TYPE 1 CAPE

TYPE 2C BOOTS

LUTHOR, LEX: No mask, bald head; green armor with detachable ultrasuit; "Lex Luthor" symbol on center of ultrasuit; purple gloves, trunks, and boots. Copyright 1988 DC Comics.

MING: Purple covered cowl on green face with black eyebrows and beard, pointed green ears; purple bodysuit with bright red and yellow detail on torso and trunks; green hands; brown boots; and purple and red Type 4 cape. Accessories included long red serpent scepter. Copyright 1988 King Features.

PENGUIN: No mask, black stovepipe hat, monicle, long pointed nose; flesh-toned obese body with white shirt, black coat with tails; purple pants with black wing tip shoes. Accessories included rainbow-colored or black umbrella. Copyright 1988 DC Comics.

PHANTOM: Purple covered cowl on flesh-toned face with black Type 1 mask; purple bodysuit was unremarkable except for black belt with silver buckle; black boots. Accessories included black whip. Copyright 1988 King Features.

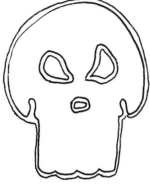

One of the Phantom's ring imprints. S. Kimball Illustration. TM King Features 1988.

RED SKULL: Type 4 red mask with skull-like features; ususaly found in green coveralls, red hands, and black boots. Accessories: any number of pistols and rifles. Copyright 1988 Marvel Comics.

RIDDLER: Black hair and magenta Type 1 mask; flesh-toned with green bodysuit with purple or black question marks over all; purple belt and gloves. Copyright 1988 DC Comics.

ROBIN: Type 2 black mask and black hair; flesh-toned with red outfit and black "Robin" symbol; yellow Type 4 cape with Type 1 collar; green trunks, boots, and gloves. Copyright 1988 DC Comics.

SPIDER-MAN: Type A (red and blue): Type 4A red mask with webbing details and large black-rimmed white eyes; red bodysuit on his torso had webbing details and small black spider on chest, blue flanked either side of the red from the middle of each pectoral muscle to the red webbing detailed belt; blue briefs and legs with red webbing detailed boots; blue arms with red webbing detailed stripe connecting from shoulder to glove which was also red webbing detailed. Accessories included Spider webbing, Spiderbuggy, and Spidercopter. Copyright 1988 Marvel Comics.

SPIDER-MAN: Type B (black and white); entire costume covered body as did Type A, but it was solid black with no webbing details; large white spider on chest and back. Accessories like those of Type A. Copyright 1988 Marvel Comics.

SUPERMAN: No mask, black hair, and blue eyes; blue bodysuit with red "Superman" symbol in center, red briefs; blue fabric legs with red boots; blue arms and bare hands. Accessories included Kryptonite and Supermobile. Copyright 1988 DC Comics.

The internationally-known Superman symbol is probably the most famous Super Hero symbol ever created. S. Kimball Illustration. TM DC Comics 1988.

THING: No mask, orange rocky head with protruding brow, small flat nose and thick rocky lips; bare rocky torso with blue fabric briefs and bare orange rocky legs and feet; bare orange rocky arms and hands. Copyright 1988 Marvel Comics.

THOR: No mask, shoulder-length blonde hair with round metallic cap that had a point on top and a large metallic wing flanking each side; large Type 2 red cape covered dark blue, torso bodysuit with four light blue filled in circles, black or brown belt, briefs had flanking light blue filled in circles; legs were black or had metallic mesh down to yellow boots which had black tapered horizontal stripes; arms were bare with red bracelets. Accessories included large, square mallet-type hammer with leather thong. Copyright 1988 Marvel Comics.

WOLVERINE: Type 3 brown mask with large black "ears" above each eye; brown bodysuit on torso with black belt and brown briefs; yellow legs with black boots with points; arms had brown torso fabric to end of tricep, bare arms with brown gloves. Accessories included a set of metallic claws (three per hand) that either extended from or connected to the back of the hands. Copyright 1988 Marvel Comics.

WONDER WOMAN: No mask, long black hair with flat, golden triangular tiara in hair; red bodysuit on torso with golden eagle, blue briefs with field of white stars, and gold belt; legs were bare to red boots with golden eagle on front of each; no gloves but golden bracelets. Accessories included golden lasso. Copyright 1988 DC Comics.

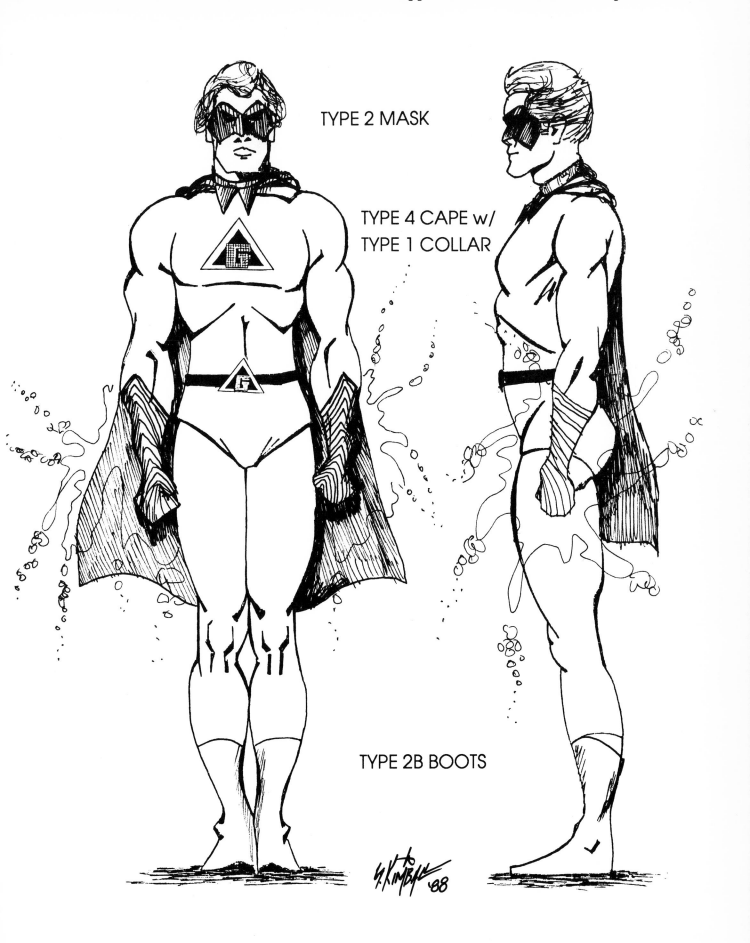

TYPE 2 MASK

TYPE 4 CAPE w/
TYPE 1 COLLAR

TYPE 2B BOOTS

Appendix II
DEALERS, COLLECTORS, and REPAIRS

*T*he following is a list of people who can help you start collecting Super Hero toys or who can help with repairs. All of those listed here are knowledgeable and have assisted the author. To reach the author, who deals in and collects all types of Super Hero memorabilia, write to: Steven H. Kimball, c/o Greenberg Publishing Company, Inc., Guide to Super Hero Toys, 7566 Main Street, Sykesville, Maryland 21784.

PRE-1960s

Danny Fuchs
209-80 18th Avenue
Bayside, New York 11360

Mikel Burton
Route 2, Box 129A
Smithville, Missouri 64089

Mike Curtis
Route 6, Box 226-00
Conway, Arkansas 72032

Joe Desris
1202 60th Street #107
Kenosha, Wisconsin 53140

Dale L. Ames
22 Colton Street
Worcester, Massachusetts 01610

CAPTAIN ACTION

John McGonagle
Box 2972
Lake Ronk, New York 11779

Jim Makowski
25 Buford Drive
Commack, New York 11725

Jim Main
125 Fort Hill Street #3
New Milford, Connecticut 06776

Craig Hedges
1416 East California Avenue
Glendale, California 91206

MEGO TOYS

Mark Huckabone
2360 West Highway 120
Grayslake, Illinois 60030

George Acevedo
3592 East Tremont
Bronx, New York 10465

SUPER POWERS

Jim Carlo
521 Ridge Road #10
Lyndhurst, New Jersey 07071

SECRET WARS

Jim Carlo
521 Ridge Road #10
Lyndhurst, New Jersey 07071

Steve Maged
22 Blondell Court
Lutherville, Maryland 21093

MAIL-ORDER AUCTION HOUSES

Ted Hake
Hake's Americana & Collectibles
P. O. Box 1444
York, Pennsylvania 17405

MAIL-ORDER CATALOGUE SALES

Other Worlds Collectibles
Frank R. Pacella
P. O. Box 4596
Bay Terrace, New York 11360-4596

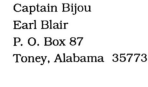

Captain Bijou
Earl Blair
P. O. Box 87
Toney, Alabama 35773

REPAIRS

Pete Dibenedetto
568 Minnesota Avenue
Buffalo, New York 14215

**Many of the doll dealers in your area can direct you to local repair shops.

The Angel (left) and Captain Marvel (SHAZAM!) (right) are both models created by Pete Debendetto. Pete creates different characters out of various parts of known Super Hero plastic models. He is highly skilled at repairing plastic toys as well.

CHARACTER INDEX
by Lari A. Kimball

*T*he following index lists every character mentioned in the book, Super Hero or not, in alphabetical order. The bold page numbers indicate a color photograph of the character.